PLAYS ONE

Philip Ridley was born in the East End of London and studied painting at St Martin's School of Art. As a writer his credits include nine children's novels – including *Krindlekrax* (1991), winner of the Smarties Prize, *Kasper in the Glitter* (1994), nominated for the Whitbread Prize, and *Scribbleboy* (1997), shortlisted for the Carnegie Medal – and two pieces for younger children. His stage plays are *The Pitchfork Disney* (1991), *The Fastest Clock in the Universe* (1992), which won the Meyer–Whitworth Prize, a *Time Out* Award, and both the Critics' Circle and the *Evening Standard* Theatre Awards for Most Promising Playwright, *Ghost from a Perfect Place* (1994), *Vincent River* (2000) and three plays for young people: *Fairytaleheart* (Hampstead Theatre, 1998), *Sparkleshark* (Royal National Theatre, 1999) and *Brokenville* (2001), which received a Fringe First nomination at the Edinburgh Festival. His short film, *The Universe of Dermot Finn* (1988), was followed by his screenplay for *The Krays* (1990), winner of the *Evening Standard* British Film of the Year Award, and the cult classic *The Reflecting Skin* (1990), which won eleven international awards and was voted one of the Best Ten Films of 1991 by the *Los Angeles Times*. In 1991 he was awarded the Most Promising Newcomer to British Film at the *Evening Standard* Film Awards. His second feature film as both writer and director, *The Passion of Darkly Noon* (1995), won the Best Director Award at the Porto Film Festival. The theme song he co-wrote for this film, 'Who Will Love Me Now?', was released as a single by P. J. Harvey. His work has been translated into seventeen languages.

PHILIP RIDLEY

Plays One

The Pitchfork Disney
The Fastest Clock in the Universe
Ghost from a Perfect Place

Introduced
by the author

faber and faber

First published in 1997 by Methuen Drama
This collection first published in 2002
by Faber and Faber Limited
3 Queen Square London WCIN 3AU
Published in the United States by Faber and Faber Inc.
an affiliate of Farrar, Straus and Giroux LLC, New York

Typeset by Country Setting, Kingsdown, Kent CT14 8ES
Printed in England by Mackays of Chatham plc, Chatham, Kent

The Pitchfork Disney first published in Great Britain in 1991
by Methuen Drama © Philip Ridley, 1991, 1997

The Fastest Clock in the Universe first published in Great Britain in 1992
by Methuen Drama © Philip Ridley, 1992, 1997

Ghost from a Perfect Place first published in Great Britain in 1994
by Methuen Drama © Philip Ridley, 1994, 1997

This collection © Philip Ridley, 2002

Introduction © Philip Ridley, 2002

A CIP record for this book is available from the British Library

0–571–21056–2

2 4 6 8 10 9 7 5 3 1

Contents

Introduction

I

Darkness.
Silence.
Then –

II

I'm being held.
I'm almost one year old.
Breath on my neck.
Mum's breath.
Dad is standing in front of the television. He's turned it on but the screen is still dark.
The machinery takes ages to warm up.
Sounds start coming from the telly: music, cheers, shouts.
Mum and Dad can hear the programme but they still can't see it.
Mum's breathing gets quicker.
Dad stares at the telly.
Then –
The screen fizzes and crackles.
The room is ablaze.
Mum cheers.
Dad cheers.
Light!

III

I'm seven years old.

I'm tucked up in bed.

I'm reading comics.

Outside: night, a car backfires, people sing in the nearby pub, something smashes, someone screams.

In the next room; muffled sound of TV, clicking of knitting-needles (Mum's making me a new balaclava), milk being poured into saucepan (Dad's making cocoa).

In this room: bedside lamp casts gentle glow over Spider-Man, Iron Man, Thor, Batman, and – my favourite comic of all – X-Men.

I feel close to all the X-Men: Cyclops, whose eyes emit a beam of light so hot it melts metal; Angel, whose clothes are specially made to conceal his vast, swan-like wings; Iceman, who can make snow by breathing on the clouds –

'I'm scared!'

It's my younger brother. A moment ago he had been asleep. But now –

'I'm scared!'

Lots of things scare him: the dark, curtains, dust in the air, slamming doors, warm pillows and – tonight's culprit – our neighbour's barking dog.

'I'm scared!'

To calm him I tell stories. This has become a sort of ritual. Each night, 'I'm scared!' Each night, 'Well, you know that empty house where the weeds are as tall as trees . . .' And another story unravels. They are about local things, faces and places we know: Mum, whose hair is so long and beautiful I'm convinced it's magic (when she cuts it I cry for hours); Dad, who can kick footballs so high I fear for satellites; Cousin Ronnie, who sets fire to insects –

'I'm scared!'

– and, sometimes, other things work their way into the stories: eyesight that can barbecue babies, angels' wings hidden so long they've become crippled and infested with maggots –

'I'm scared!'

– distant cousins who eat burnt butterflies because it's the only way to stop their magic breath turning clouds to snow –

'I'm scared!'

– another story –

'I'm scared!'

– story.

IV

'Look at this one!'

'Wow – it's huge!'

'Tarantula size.'

'Where's the jar?'

'Here!'

'Put it in, Phil!'

'Open it, Tel.'

'Fuck! We've got millions and millions.'

'Yeah! But we want more!'

'More!'

'More!'

All day me and Terry, my best mate, have been filling an old pickle jar with spiders, beetles, ladybirds, cockroaches, anything that crawls and wriggles.

'Look, Phil!'

'Fuck! What is it?'

'Dunno! It's all green and –'

'In the jar!'

'More!'

'More!'

This derelict house is a bug hunter's paradise. Rotten stairs reveal woodlice by the handful. Kicking an old mattress erupts an exodus of nameless wildlife.

'Look, Tel.'

'Worm!'

'Nah! Centipede.'

'Jar!'

'More!'

'More!'

Summer sunlight blazes through cracked windows and holes in the roof. The air is syrup-heavy and buzzes with flies.

'Look . . . Phil! Look!'

Terry has put the jar on a window sill and is sitting cross-legged in front of it.

I go over and see –

Ants attacking spiders. Centipedes curling round beetles. Like a multicoloured liquid bubbling to the boil.

And the sunlight sparkles on the glass, making rainbow colours, and the beetles glisten like emeralds, ladybirds like rubies . . . oh, this is our treasure of glorious violence.

We stare, riveted.

The sunlight turns amber as the day wears on. And still we stare at our own private Armageddon.

We gasp as legs are severed.

We thrill at decapitation.

'More!'

'More!'

V

Ten minutes later.

A large spider crawls up the wall and across the window sill. Its body's the size of my thumbnail. Tiny hairs on its legs. It scarpers up to the glass jar, then stops, as if studying the carnage within.

'The King Spider,' says Terry.

'Yesss!'

'It must fight!'

'Yesss!'

Terry goes to catch the spider but it scurries away.

'Coward!'

'Yesss! Yesss!'

'The King Spider must be executed for cowardice!'

'Yesss!'

Terry gets a penknife from his pocket, flicks it open and stabs at the spider.

'Missed!' I cry.

Terry stabs again.

'Missed!'

'Trying to escape means . . . torture!'

'Yesss!'

The spider is manoeuvred to the middle of the window sill.

I press its body with my little finger, pinning it into position.

Terry says, 'The King Spider is supposed to be the bravest of all spiders. It has shown cowardice by running away and then trying to avoid punishment. According to the law of the land it must have two legs cut off. This will make it an insect.'

'Oh, yesss!'

Terry holds the point of the blade above one of the spider's legs.

I say, 'Let punishment commence.'
And –
Cut!
A leg is severed.
The spider doesn't move.
'Let punishment commence!'
Cut!
Another leg.
I lift my finger. The spider tries to crawl away but seems fazed by the loss of two limbs. It goes round in circles.
'More legs!'
'Yesss!'
The blade does its work until the spider is legless. Faint twitching can be detected for a moment, then stops.
Terry and I peer as close as we can.
'Is it dead?' asks Terry.
I press my finger against the body until it goes pop.
'It is now,' I say.
We look at each other and grin. We're both flushed with lethal thrill. We look at the spiders in the jar.
'More torture!'
'Yessssssss!'

VI

One hour later.
Terry has gone home.
I'm alone with the jar.
I walk up the rickety stairs to the abandoned bedroom. The shattered windows are ablaze with setting sunlight. It illuminates the bed (with burnt mattress) and a dressing-table (with cracked mirror).
I open one of the dressing-table drawers and discover old make-up: a compact, lipstick, glittery eyeshadow and

a hairbrush with long grey hairs stuck in the bristles.
Another drawer reveals a box full of needles and thread.

Carefully, I thread a needle. Then open the jar of
insects. I get a ladybird and stick the needle right
through it.

Then another ladybird.

A beetle.

An earwig.

One by one I spear the tiny creatures, my fingertips
moist with blood (like I've been picking berries), until
the length of cotton is a necklace of wriggling things.

I tie it round my neck.

I unscrew the lipstick and smear it across my mouth.
I rub glittery eyeshadow on my eyelids.

I stare at my reflection.

The cracked mirror shatters my face into a hundred
pieces.

The legs of the insects wriggle and tickle my skin.

My lips are a slash of blood.

My eyes glint and sparkle.

I am a wild thing in a wild kingdom.

Look at me!

Oh, look at me!

This is what I truly am!

VII

I am eight years old but I feel ancient. I like to hurt
harmless things. I like the feel of blood on my fingertips.
I like to drop beetles into bleach. I like the way their skin
bursts like a flower in bloom. I like to cut up worms and
burn pigeons and shoot baby rabbits with air rifles.

I like this derelict house. It is my kingdom. My world.
I like the broken windows and the cracked brickwork
and the photos of strangers still hanging on walls and

the layers of wallpaper like peeling skin. I like the smell. I like the dead cat with maggots in its belly.

I am happy here.

I like walking from ruined room to ruined room, with my insect necklace and my red lips and gold eyelids and blood on my fingers and my dreams of decay.

I want to live here for ever. I want to take my clothes off and roll in the dirt. I want to wear nettles and weeds in my hair and drink rainwater and bite the heads from rats.

I'll stab anyone who tries to tame me. I'll impale them like I impaled the fucking insects. I'll cut off their ears and make a necklace of them. I'll use their severed scrotums to keep my sherbet in. I'll use the tops of their skulls as bowls for my cornflakes.

I'm a monster, me.

A monster, me.

Monster, me.

Monster.

VIII

I'm nine years old.

I'm at school.

My class has been asked to write about what we did over the weekend. I can tell by their faces everyone hates the idea. Most of them have struggled through a grudging two or three lines. But me . . . oh, I can't write fast enough. I've already covered four sides and would have carried on were it not for –

'All right, boys,' says Mr Edwards, my teacher. 'Who wants to read theirs first? Terry, what about you?'

Terry reads a story about taking his dog for a walk.

'Very good – Mark, you next!'

Mark went shopping with his mum.

'Philip – you!'

I jump to my feet and launch into, 'On Saturday I went down the market all by myself. I watched the man on the eel stall. The eels are kept in big metal trays. They are alive. Wriggling and shiny and black. The man who works at the eel stall wears a white overall. I like it best when he kills an eel. He chops it up while it's still alive. The little chunks of eel keep on wriggling for a while. They are very red inside. I don't see any bone. Sometimes the blood spurts all over the white overall –'

'That's quite enough!' interrupts Mr Edwards. 'I want you to write two hundred lines: "If I've got nothing nice to say, it's best to say nothing."'

IX

I'm ten years old.

Saturday night.

The pub at the end of the street – The Temple Tap – has just emptied.

This can only mean one thing: A Drunken Fight!

I look out of the window, waiting.

Listening . . .

Then –

Yells!

Screams!

Smashing glass!

Running footsteps!

My heart is beating very fast.

It's the most exciting moment of the week.

I can't wait for the morning to see blood in the gutter.

X

Carefully, I cut the photograph from a magazine. It's part of a double-page spread. There's a crease going down the middle where the magazine folded. Also, some slightly frayed staple holes.

Snip, snip!

The photograph is black and white. A cityscape. Or, rather, what used to be a cityscape. Now there's only one house left. Everything else, for as far as the eye can see, has been destroyed. Burnt and flattened.

Snip, snip!

A few objects can be discerned in the rubble: a bicycle . . . an umbrella perhaps . . . a doll . . .

Snip, snip!

. . . a scorched tree claws at the pure white sky . . .

Snip!

There! All done!

I smooth the photograph on the table in front of me.

Mum walks by and looks over my shoulder. 'Oh, what you looking at that for?' she asks with a shudder. 'It's so morbid. So ugly.'

But I don't find it ugly at all.

For me there's something beautiful and peaceful in the inhuman, humanless devastation. And that solitary house! Imagine being in there when the bomb was dropped. To look out of the window and see your world evaporate.

Somehow, the thought appeals.

'Put it away,' Mum tells me irritably. 'A boy your age should be out playing.'

I'm eleven years old and my favourite photograph is of Hiroshima.

XI

I'm twelve years old.

It's Sunday morning.

I'm sipping fizzy grapefruit juice and looking at apple turnovers and jam doughnuts.

Every Sunday Dad takes me and my brother to Victoria Park while Mum does the housework and prepares the roast dinner. The routine never changes: me and my brother get dressed in our Sunday best, Dad says, 'Come on, boys!' at exactly eleven o'clock, we all get in the car, Dad drives us to the park and we all stroll around the flower garden (we do this even in winter when there are no flowers), we walk to the lake and feed the ducks, we play frisbee until Dad asks –

'Thirsty, boys?'

'Yeah!' I say.

'Yeah!' says my brother.

We walk to the small canteen and Dad asks –

'What d'you want, boys?'

'Fizzy grapefruit.'

'Fizzy cherry.'

Dad buys the drinks and sees us looking longingly at the cakes.

'Nothing to eat, boys,' Dad says. 'It'll ruin your dinner and –'

A scream!

Glass smashing!

Yells and shouts and –

Feathers!

The air is full of white feathers.

A swan has swallowed a fish hook! It's flapping and hissing. A man is clutching his fishing-rod. He won't let go. The swan has become a monstrous kite of pain and –

Crash!

The swan is moving away from the lake. Picnicking couples dash for cover. Flasks smash. A wastepaper basket is knocked over. The swan is like a loose propeller and the man is still clutching his fishing-rod and yelling and feathers fall like snowflakes and –

Pink!

The hook is pulling something pink, like wet silk, from deep inside the swan. I see the pink wetness get longer and longer, speckles of blood appear, as the swan – its wings punching the air – gets closer . . .

Closer . . .

Closer . . .

Plastic chairs are knocked over. A woman screams. I feel my Dad's hand squeeze my shoulder. A bottle smashes. The air is full of shrieks and feathers and –

Silence!

The swan frees itself.

Flies away.

The man walks back to the lake with his fishing-rod. Picnickers resume picnicking. Dad's hand leaves my shoulder. I swallow my fizzy grapefruit juice.

'– your Mum'll be upset if you don't eat your dinner,' finishes Dad.

XII

I'm drowning.

Water explodes in my lungs. Roars in my ears. Dirty, dark, cold water. How did I get here? Where is here? Am I in an ocean? I'm sure I was safe until very recently. I was somewhere familiar. Somewhere with lots of air –

The pain!

My chest is bursting and my windpipe is constricting and the sound of my breathing wakes me up –

'Keep calm, Phil.'

'Don't panic, son.'

Mum and Dad are beside the bed.

My brother stares, petrified.

The luminous clock says 4.30.

I'm having an asthma attack.

I'm wet with sweat. It's like I've just run the marathon and I'm breathing through straw . . . and the straw is closing . . . closing . . .

'Keep calm.'

'Don't panic.'

I stare at the luminous stars I've stuck to the ceiling. I imagine I'm in a space capsule with an endless supply of oxygen. I'm floating in oblivion. No one can harm me. No one can beat me up at school. No one can torment me. I don't belong to anyone. No one belongs to me.

I'm alone in space.

I'm alone in space.

I'm alone in space . . .

'That's better,' says Mum.

'Good boy,' says Dad.

I'm alone . . .

I'm alone . . .

'Breathe –'

Alone!

'– deep!'

Alone . . .

XIII

Faces and voices are distorted.

I stare at everyone through the opaque plastic of an oxygen tent. Everything's blurred and muffled and not quite real.

This is my bedroom – but not my bedroom.

That's my brother – but not my brother.

Here's my pile of comics – but not my pile of comics.

People talk as if the plastic is soundproofed or I'm brain-dead.

'Oh, he never complains!' says Mum to Aunt Rita. 'So long as he's got a pencil and paper he's happy as a sandboy. He can read a book a day. He loves horror stuff. Look at his left eye! He burst a blood vessel trying to breathe.'

You don't know it, dear Mum and Auntie, but I'm writing down everything you say. You don't flinch when I stare at you. Because of this oxygen tent I notice things I would never have noticed. I hear things I would never have heard.

This distorting plastic has made the world terrifyingly clear.

XIV

I love the blood congealed in my eye. I love the way people go 'Ugh' when they see it. I love my sickly pale skin. I love the way you can see veins through this pale skin. I love the way you can see blood pump in the veins visible in my pale skin. I love the way people go 'Ugh' when they see it. I love the way my scratches and spots take ages to heal. I love the way they bleed 'n' scab, bleed 'n' scab, bleed 'n' scab. I love the way people go 'Ugh' when they see them. I love the dark rings under my eyes. I love the way they make me look older. I love the way they make me look beaten up. I like the tiny blood vessels in the dark rings. I like the way people go 'Ugh' when they see them. I love the yellow fur on my tongue. I love my cracked dry lips. I love my breath that stinks of foul medicine. I love the way people go 'Ugh' when they smell it. I love my thin body. I love the bony rib-cage and the muscleless arms and the withered legs and the wire-coat-hanger shoulders. I love the way people go 'Ugh' when they see them. I love the way I stoop when I walk. I love the way I wheeze when I talk. I love all the things asthma does to me.

Sickness has turned me into poetry.

XV

Spider-Man says, 'I love the way you look too, kid. In fact, you're one of the most beautiful kids I've ever seen – Heck! I know a guy ain't supposed to refer to another guy as beautiful but . . . well, we're good mates, ain't we? Sure we are! You've read everything I've done since I was first bitten by the radioactive spider. You know, I bet there's things about me you know that *I'm* not even aware of. So . . . well, if I want to say you're beautiful then I think I'm fully entitled to do so. After all, we're on intimate terms. We should trust each other. I trust you. You trust me. Spider-Man and Phil – best mates for ever, eh? Can I get into that oxygen tent with you? Thanks . . . Mmmm, it's cosy in here . . . You know, there are some people who'll tell you I'm just a figment of your imagination. They'll say, "He's just a comic-book character! How can you see him in your bedroom!" Well, I say, real is as real does! So . . . can you feel that? My hand on your knee? There! I *must* be real then . . . What about if I put my hand here – Oooo, are you getting a hard-on, beautiful boy? I think you are. Oh, no, I don't mind. I'm thrilled. Just let it happen, my sweet bloodshot-eyed kid. Here – let me get your cock out of your pyjamas for you! Wow! That *is* big! No, no, don't you do anything. You just close your eyes and let your friendly neighbourhood Spider-Man do all the work . . . I'll just rub it for you like this . . . Wow! If my Auntie May could see me now, eh? You enjoying that? I bet you are. Oh, look at your hips thrusting. Listen to your breath rasping. I'll rub you faster . . . Faster! Faster! Harder! Hard – ooo, look at all that spunk spurting! It's gone all over my costume! It looks like my web fluid. Is that your first spunk . . .? It is! Well, you're nearly thirteen, so it's about time. Congratulations, blood-eyed beauty. And listen to your Spidey – don't let anyone tell you this ain't real!'

XVI

One year later.

Victoria Park. Sunday morning. Fizzy grapefruit.

We've walked away from the canteen and are watching local footballers. I'm standing next to my brother who yells –

'Offside!'

Dad says, 'Yeah, you're right, son.'

I've no idea what they're talking about. I've got no interest in football whatsoever. All I'm watching is –

Him!

He's about seventeen years old and he's wearing very tight shorts and he's got jet-black hair and very thick eyebrows and . . . oh, he reminds me of someone! Who? Who? I watch him kick the football and spit and scratch his crotch and –

Captain Scarlet!

Of course! He looks like Captain Scarlet. My favourite

puppet show. Nothing can harm Captain Scarlet. Bullets bounce off him. He walks away from car crashes and burning buildings. He's indestructible!

And he's playing football right in front of me.

I can't take my eyes off him.

The game finishes.

Crowds disperse.

I watch Captain Scarlet as he walks towards a car with some mates.

I walk after him. I walk without knowing I'm walking. I watch him open a car door and throw his sports bag on the back seat. I watch him wipe his face with a towel. I watch him lean against the bonnet and drink a Coke. I watch him slap someone on the back and say, 'Nice one.' I watch him comb his hair and bite a Mars bar. I watch him lean into the car and turn the radio on. I watch him tap his foot to a song I don't know –

'Phil!'

I turn to see Dad a surprising distance away.

'Come here!' calls Dad.

Slowly, sipping fizzy grapefruit, I return to Dad.

'Don't go wandering off,' says Dad. 'D'you wanna get lost or something?'

XVII

Three weeks later.

Sunday.

Park.

Juice.

We're feeding the deer stale bread. The deer are in a special, fenced-off enclosure. I like the roughness of their tongues. I like the way the baby ones jump when I yell 'Boo!'

'I need to go for a wee, Dad,' I say.

'Can't you wait until we get home?'

'Nah.'

Dad tuts and we move round to the other side of the deer (the side we never go to) so I can pop into the public toilets.

'Don't take long,' says Dad.

I walk down the little path. The gravel crunches and birds sing. The smell of disinfectant and piss gets stronger.

I step into the toilet –

White tiles.

Wet leaves on the floor.

And Captain Scarlet.

There he is! Standing at the urinal! He's wearing sky-blue jeans and a white T-shirt and his hair . . . oh, what a quiff. I've never seen hair so sculptured, so gravity-defying, so gleaming.

Captain Scarlet turns to look at me.

I'm frozen to the spot. There's just me and him and the sound of trickling water and the smell of bleach and the birds singing in the trees outside and –

Captain Scarlet is clutching his cock.

It's stiff and very red, like a beakless vulture head, and he's rubbing it, slowly, firmly, and looking at me and smiling and –

I can't move.

I can't do anything.

I just stare at Captain Scarlet as he rubs his cock faster and faster.

And he's still smiling at me. But now his face is turning really red and it's gleaming with sweat and his vulture head is turning wet and making squishy noises like it's chewing gum and the birds are tweeting outside and my heart's going boom and –

Captain Scarlet shoots spunk!

It spurts across the tiled floor.

One gob lands on my left shoe.

Captain Scarlet puts his cock away, zips himself up and winks at me.

I try to wink back.

Captain Scarlet walks up to me, ruffles my hair . . . then leaves.

I look at the spunk on my shoe. It looks like Mum's hair conditioner.

I leave it there while I piss.

I leave it there while I go back to the deer and Dad says, 'You took your time. I was about to send a search party.'

I leave it there while I feed more stale bread to animals who look so frightened when I yell, 'Boo!'

XVIII

The dead kid is the same age as me. He's wearing a black suit and a black tie. His shoes are very shiny. The soles of the shoes are smooth and spotless. His fingers are laced together. There's a gold ring on the little finger of his left hand. His hair is so black and so neat and it looks like a –

'It's a wig,' Simon tells me.

'Yeah, I thought so.'

We're standing beside a coffin in a funeral parlour. It's two o'clock in the morning and we're studying the corpse by torchlight. We're talking in whispers and – due to the December cold – shivering.

'Cancer,' says Simon.

'Eh?'

'The wig. Radiation made his hair fall out. His parents wanted the wig. Dad says it makes him look like a midget Roy Orbison.'

Simon's dad is an undertaker. It's his job to make the corpses look as healthy and lifelike as possible.

'Time to touch, Phil.'

'Yeah, yeah.'

I've stayed over at Simon's lots of times. We always creep downstairs in the middle of the night to view a corpse (or, if I'm lucky, corpses). Touching them started as a sort of dare. But – as neither of us had been particularly fazed – it's now more of a ritual.

I touch the dead kid's forehead.

Simon touches the dead kid's forehead.

'Let's go back up,' he whispers. 'I'm freezing!'

I touch the dead kid's lips.

'Phil! Come on! Enough.'

I'm touching the dead kid's neck.

I'm touching the dead kid's shirt.

I'm undoing the dead kid's shirt.

'What you fucking up to?'

'It's all right!'

'Dad'll go ape-shit if you mess up –'

'Shhhh!'

I undo another button on the dead kid's shirt. I need to see some skin. I need to see –

I pull the dead kid's shirt open.

Another button.

Pull and –

There!

A nipple! Dark and flat like a chocolate button.

I touch the nipple of the dead kid.

It feels like a pencil eraser.

'Phil!'

'Okay, okay.'

I do the buttons back up.

Smooth the shirt flat.

We creep back upstairs.

Simon gets into his bed and I snuggle into the sleeping-bag on the floor.

'Chocolate?' asks Simon, breaking a chunk from the bar on his bedside cabinet.

'Mmmm,' I say. 'I'm starving.'

XIX

I'm fourteen.

It's a cold, November evening.

I'm walking down Hackney Road. I've just bought a kebab and I'm picking at it through a hole in the wrapping paper.

I stand at the zebra crossing.

A car stops.

I raise my hand in thanks as I step out –

The car starts up!

Aims straight at me!

I jump back. Stumble. Drop my kebab. And crack my spine painfully on the kerb.

A car window winds down.

A middle-aged man looks at me. Another man, younger, is driving. I've never seen either of them before. They're both wearing baseball caps and they're breathing very fast.

'You're a lucky bastard,' says the middle-aged man, stabbing his finger at me (I count three gold sovereigns, plus a gold bracelet and the beginning of a tattoo peeking beneath his black tracksuit top). 'We fucking hate you! We took one look at you and we hate your fucking guts.' He nudges his mate. 'Don't we, eh?'

'Yeah,' says the younger bloke.

'We were gonna run you over and leave you to fucking die in the gutter like you fucking deserve.'

'I ain't never seen you before!' I find myself crying.

'Don't push it, you cunt, don't push it!' Middle-Aged Man is rattling the lock of the door. 'Honest, I'm on the verge of kicking your fucking head in. I just don't like the fucking look of you. I wanna puke when I see you. We both do, don't we, mate?'

'Yeah, yeah,' agrees Younger Bloke. 'He's fucking shit. Slime! Let's knife him.'

'Nah, I'm bored now,' Middle-Aged Bloke says. Then glares at me. 'Just pray our fucking paths don't ever fucking cross again, you cunt.'

The car drives off.

I get to my feet. My spine is throbbing. Bits of kebab stuck to my jeans.

I'm still shaking when I get home.

Mum says, 'You ain't eaten a whole kebab already, have you?'

'I . . . er . . . didn't buy one in the end,' I tell her. 'Not hungry.'

Mum says, 'Ooo, you're such a fibber. I can smell it on you.'

XX

There's a dead bird in the road outside. I can see it from the living-room window. Squashed on the tarmac. Red and grey. Blood and feathers. It's been there for three days. Cars keep going over it. But it won't go away. It just gets flatter and flatter. It's part of the road now. I can't stop thinking about it. I have to walk over this bird on my way to school. I have to walk over this bird on my way home from school. I can't help studying it. If I look hard enough I can see the shape of its head. A wing. A claw. Tiny bones amongst the red and the grey. When I close my eyes I see the dead bird. Like it's imprinted on my retina. Will it always be there? Will I always see this dead bird? And why hasn't anyone else mentioned it? How can Mum and Dad get on with life as if everything's normal? Don't they know there's a dead bird right outside our front door? Don't they know you can see it from the living-room window? Am I the only one that's bothered to be living so close to feathers and blood?

XXI

'"Once, long ago, there was a handsome Prince –"'

'Poof!'

'Shut up, Krafer,' warns Mr Williams. 'Go on, Ridley.'

It's an English lesson at school. One by one we've been reading last night's homework: a story (any subject matter) demonstrating a moment of climax. ('When a story reaches its climax,' Mr. Williams had explained, 'you must use shorter sentences.')

I continue, '"Everyone in the Castle thought the Prince was the most beautiful thing they had ever seen. Everyone swooned when they saw him and said, 'Oh, look at the Prince! He is more beautiful than a million swans flying across a sunset. More beautiful than a million butterflies in a field of orchids. And more beautiful than a million unicorns frolicking in the surf.' And the Prince thought he was beautiful too –"'

'Poof.'

'Shut it, Middleburg. Go on, Ridley.'

I continue, '"One day, the King returned from a distant battle. He brought the spoils of war back to the Castle. There was jewellery made of platinum, swords made of silver and statues made of ivory. There was also . . . a strange bird –"'

'Poof!'

'Shut up, Newman. Go on, Ridley.'

'"The Prince said, 'Look at that silly-looking bird. Its long tail-feathers drag in the mud! Ha!' And everyone in the Castle laughed with the beautiful Prince. The Prince put a lead round the bird's neck and took it for walks round the Castle. And everyone said, 'Oh, look! There goes the beautiful Prince with that silly-looking bird.' But then . . . a strange thing happened. The bird's tail feathers opened up into a magnificent display. So many colours! Red, yellow, blue, amber. All whirling and swirling together. And everyone in the Castle gasped and said, 'Look at the bird! It is more beautiful than a million swans flying across the sunset. More beautiful than a million butterflies in a field of orchids. More beautiful than a million unicorns frolicking in the surf. And it's definitely more beautiful than the Prince.'"

'It's a peacock,' says Krafer.

'Yeah,' says Middleburg.

'Yeah,' says Newman.

'Go on, Ridley.'

'"The Prince hated not being the most beautiful thing in the Castle. So, that night, when everyone was asleep, he got a blowtorch! He crept into the tower where the bird was kept. He lit the flame of the blowtorch. The flame was bright red. Lots of colours. He approached the bird. He aimed the flame at the bird's head. Feathers crackled. Eyes popped. The bird shrieked –"'

'STOP!' yells Mr Williams. He glares at me. He's trembling with anger. 'You bring this on yourself,' he snarls, approaching me. 'The way the class hates you. You provoke it. You don't even meet them half-way. You don't *try* to fit in. You're not a team-player, Ridley. You know that? You'll always be exactly what you are now. Sitting alone in the corner and despised!'

XXII

If I've got nothing nice to say, it's best to say nothing.
If I've got nothing nice to say, it's best to say nothing.
If I've got nothing nice to say, it's best to say nothing.
If I've got nothing nice to say, it's best to say nothing.
If I've got nothing nice to say, it's best to say nothing.
If I've got nothing nice to say, it's best to say nothing.
If I've got nothing nice to say, it's best to say nothing.

XXIII

I wish I could be in a car crash. Trapped for hours in twisted metal. Firemen struggling to free me. My brave face, speckled with blood, valiantly trying to smile as they amputate my left leg below the knee. Cheers from onlookers as I'm pulled from the wreck. I wave at them and, again, attempt a smile. A medic dabs sweat from my forehead as I'm put in an ambulance. A needle is thrust into my vein. I become groggy with pain-killers. I hear someone say, 'It's a shame about his leg. So young. So attractive.' I call out, 'I was never good at dancing anyway,' and everyone's eyes brim with tears at my courage. I try to crack jokes as the ambulance – siren blaring, tyres screeching – speeds to hospital. I'm stretchered into intensive care. More tubes are thrust into my veins and up my nose and . . . . oh, I need this to happen. Don't you see? I need something dramatic to happen in my fucking life. I need something to help me become the centre, the focus, to prove what I am. I need a car crash, for fuck's sake. Is that too much to ask? Just a simple fucking car crash?

XXIV

I've got nothing nice to say, it's best to say.
I've got nothing nice to say, it's best to say.
I've got nothing nice to say, it's best to say.
I've got nothing nice to say, it's best to say.
I've got nothing nice to say, it's best to say.

XXV

Or cancer. I need a tumour somewhere in my gut. Or brain! Yeah! Even better! The doctor says, 'You'll need chemotherapy and radiation treatment. You're going to feel very ill for a very long time and, even then, you might not make it.' I say, 'I'm not afraid, Doc. I'm gonna lick this thing.' Mum and Dad are blubbering as they check me into hospital. Mum says, 'Do you need anything?' I reply, 'Just a pen and paper. That's all I've ever needed, ain't it, Mum?' And her tears become overwhelming and she embraces me. The chemotherapy makes me vomit and sweat. I lose weight. Radiation makes my hair fall out. I become very, very weak. But still – every moment I'm not vomiting or too feverish – I'm writing. Writing the greatest prose a sick teenager ever put to paper. When friends visit they can't conceal their shock at my appearance. They gasp out loud. One or two look close to fainting. I say, 'I was no oil painting anyway.' And they all hug me and tell me how I've always been an inspiration, never more so than now. Months go by like this. Until, finally, the tumour is shrivelled to nothing and I'm discharged. I walk through the hospital gates with Mum and Dad at my side and my finished masterwork under my arm. Outside, other family members (distant cousins and great-great aunts

I never knew I had) and friends (even long lost friends
I never thought I'd see again) cheer and clap. There's a
news crew. A microphone is thrust under my nose. I'm
on telly. Planes zoom by in a celebratory fly-past. One
sky-writes, 'WE LOVE PHIL!' Traffic comes to a halt.
Publishers offer me contracts. My life story is to be
filmed . . . Oh, I need this to happen! How else can
I prove myself? I need to survive a serious illness, for
fuck's sake. Is that too much to ask? A simple tumour?

XXVI

Nothing nice to say is best.
Nothing nice to say is best.
Nothing nice to say is best.

XXVII

Or a savage attack. Someone tries to kill me. Yeah!
I'm . . . I'm walking home late at night. Minding my
own business. Then, without warning, a shadowy figure.
A flash of a blade. Knife in my gut. Wetness spreads over
my T-shirt and down my legs. I try to fight back but my
attacker is much, much stronger. A crazy psycho. I'm
stabbed again and again. I'm left for dead in the gutter.
I cry for help. No one comes. I crawl all the way down
Bethnal Green Road, leaving a trail of blood behind
me. My bloodied hand reaches up and knocks on my
front door. Mum looks out of the window above and,
'Ahhhhhhhh!!!!' An ambulance is called. Hospital. Seven
hours of surgery. I'm lucky to survive. Afterwards I lie
in bed, pale, wrapped in bandages, tubes up my nose and
down my throat and I – oh, fuck! Listen! I need to be
nearly murdered. Surely that ain't too much to ask, eh?

People get attacked every second of the fucking day. Why not me? Eh? Why should I remain unscathed when surrounded by such random butchery?

XXVIII

I say nothing nice.

XXIX

I'm fifteen.

It's Saturday night.

Nearly midnight.

I'm standing alone outside 'CHERRY'S DISCO'.

I've never actually been *inside* the disco. But most people in my class have. They come here in a big crowd every weekend. They're not old enough to get in but . . . well, when they're suited 'n' booted and got a girl-friend in tow, they could pass for eighteen. Easy. The bouncers don't ask any questions.

I'm standing on the other side of the car park, watching from a distance, as –

There they are!

My classmates! Well, not actually *mates*.

I haven't really got anyone in class I know well enough to call a mate. Oh, sure, I talk to a few people but . . . well, we don't see each other outside school. They don't sit in my bedroom (or me in theirs) and listen to records or watch telly or sit in that comfortable silence I hear so much about. That's why I'm standing all alone while a crowd of boys from my class are –

There!

Strolling along together. Cracking jokes. Already a bit drunk. Having a good time.

Oh, what must it be like?

What are they feeling? Eh? Eh?

What must it be like to be part of a crowd like that? To be so relaxed with other people, share in-jokes and a bottle of beer, wear those 'in-crowd' clothes, snog in front of mates, dance in front of mates, buy drinks for mates, have mates buy drinks for you –

Sound of cheering!

Laughter!

People from my class slip into the disco.

What must it be like in there? The music's so loud it's making my teeth vibrate even at this distance.

What must it be like?

What?

After a while I make my way home. It's a bit of a trek. The disco is right out at Hackney Stadium and I've got to walk round Victoria Park, then down Cassland Road, then Mare Street, then Cambridge Heath Road and –

Ouch!

Something in my shoe. I take it off and see a piece of broken glass. It's gone right through my sole. Carefully, using my keys, I start to pick it out.

The keys rattle. I'm breathing heavily, murmuring in concentration. Hopping on my one shoe'd foot.

Rattling.

Breathing.

Hopping.

Then –

I glance up and notice an old woman gazing at me through her living-room window.

For a moment we just stare at each other.

Then I say, 'Glass in my shoe. I'm getting it out.'

The old woman gives a chuckle and nods, 'Oh! That's it, is it!' she says. 'I've been watching and watching and . . . well, I *did* wonder.'

XXX

I hate summer. I hate blue skies with no prospect of rain. I hate the way birds tweet and dogs chase frisbees. I hate gardens full of flowers and lawns chock-a-block with sunbathers. I hate the way boys wear T-shirts with big smiley faces on them. I hate the way girls wear T-shirts with big smiley faces on them. I hate the way boys and girls have big smiles on their own smiley faces. I hate the way a boy's smiley face meets a girl's smiley face and they're both so pleased with each other's smiliness. I hate the way they hold hands, gulp fizzy drinks, gyrate to pop songs, laugh, canoodle. I hate the way they say, 'I love you,' without mentioning serial killers once. I hate their gratuitous optimism. I hate their pornographic display of pleasure. I hate the way they can just abandon themselves to joy without worrying about a plane crashing on them or a bomb going off or a mad gunman shooting holes in their smiling faces. I hate the way, when the sun shines, they see nothing but a sunny day.

XXXI

I'm sixteen.

I'm in my classroom at school. It's the first day of the new academic year. I'm in the Lower Sixth year now. Most of the boys who used to be in my class have gone. They left after taking their O-Levels last July. Only the boys studying A-Levels remain. That's me and sixteen others.

One of them is Keith.

Keith is one of the boys I used to watch going into 'Cherry's'. He was one of the loudest, the drunkest, the best dancer (or so I've heard others say), the first to get a steady girlfriend. But now -

Keith sits very quietly. His mates keep a distance. They don't laugh or joke around him. When they do approach, it's gently, almost on tiptoes, as if Keith's wired with dynamite and might explode at the slightest turbulence.

Keith's mum has just died.

I knew nothing about it until this morning. And I've only managed to pick up the odd whispered word . . .

'Cancer.' 'Suffered.' 'Tragic.'

The bell goes for first lesson.

Keith's mates rush out, glad to get away.

Slowly, Keith stands and picks up his books. He looks over at me and smiles, 'All right?'

'Yeah,' I say.

'It's like I've got the plague or something.'

'Yeah.'

'It's just me old dear dead. That's all. It happens.'

'Yeah. But it . . . happened to you first.'

'Yeah.'

'Cancer, was it?'

'Leukaemia.'

'What's that exactly?'

'Sort of cancer of the blood.'

'Does it just . . . happen?'

'Oh, yeah. You can't catch it or anything. It's natural.'

'Naturally unlucky, eh?'

'Yeah.' Keith laughs and comes over to me. 'You know, the day before she copped it . . . I was in hospital with her . . . The screens were all around. Mum was asleep. And I opened her nightdress. I looked at her tits. Then I got up onto the bed and . . . I just started to suck one of her nipples. You know? Like I was a baby or something. And it didn't seem weird or wrong or anything.'

'Did any milk or stuff come out?'

'Oh, nah, nah.'

'Did you get a hard-on?'

'Nah! For fuck's sake . . . you're weirder than me.' He grins. 'Thank God!'

XXXII

Nine months later.

I'm at Keith's flat.

It's Saturday evening.

We're going to 'Cherry's'.

We've been going nearly every Saturday for the past few months. It's a pricey night out (what with the entrance fee, money for drinks – rip-off prices – and, usually, a taxi home) but, as Keith has got a part-time job in a pie-and-mash shop and I've got a part-time job at the local cinema, we're both loaded with pocket money.

I'm in the garden with Keith's dad, Bill. It has been a warm day and Bill's tending some flowers.

Keith is upstairs in his bedroom still titivating himself.

'First year I've had to deal with all this,' Bill tells me, indicating the herbaceous border. 'This was my other-half's domain.'

I say, 'Oh, yeah, right.'

'She had green fingers. Not me. The rose bushes are a mess. I didn't know you had to prune them in March or something. I've just let them grow. Look at 'em.'

'They're . . . bushy.'

'*Too* bushy. That's the problem. By the time the summer really takes off . . . well, it'll be a bloody jungle out here. I never realised how much work she put in. To the garden. I never realised all the hours she must've . . .'

And, suddenly, he's crying.

Standing in the middle of the garden, clutching a trowel, his fingernails thick with earth, and blubbering.

I stare.

I stare at his trembling hands, his belly muscles heaving, the way a vein throbs in his neck, his twitching lips, the saliva on his chin, the way he tries to swallow, the gurgling sound this makes, the snot running from his nose, the tears running down his cheeks, his bloodshot eyes, the sweat on his forehead, the sweat mixing with snot, the snot and sweat mixing with saliva, the whimpering noises, strangely musical, like wind through guitar strings –

'Dad! For fuck's sake! Belt up!'

Keith walks into the garden and glares angrily at his dad.

Bill tries to stop crying, but can't.

'Come on, Phil.' Keith tugs at my sleeve. 'He's fucking embarrassing when he gets like this. Come on.'

We walk out of the flat.

Outside Keith says, 'I'm sorry about that.'

'Don't be,' I tell him. 'It was . . . fascinating.'

XXXIII

Four hours later.

We're standing in line, waiting to get into 'Cherry's'.

It's exceptionally busy tonight and most people – including me and Keith – are already pretty drunk.

Keith passes me the bottle of vodka we've been swigging from. 'Best finish it quick,' he says. 'They won't let us take it in.'

I take a swig.

Keith takes a swig.

I take a –

'Ahhh!'

A cry from a bloke behind us. He's clutching his left buttock.

'What's up with you?' his girlfriend asks.

The man looks at his hand. It's covered with blood.

'Those bastards –' And suddenly he rushes off. Across the car park. He's chasing a couple of blokes.

We hear laughter and jeering.

Keith nudges me in the ribs. 'He's been Stanley-knifed.'

'Yeah,' I say.

A Stanley knife in the buttocks is a regular event at 'Cherry's'.

Stabbed Man returns, breathless, sweating, blood staining his trousers. 'Fuck me,' he laughs. 'The cunts, eh?'

'Did you get 'em?' asks someone.

'Nah! Fuck me – Look! Trousers ruined. I'm bleeding all over the cunting joint.'

'You need stitches in that,' says someone.

'Yeah! C'mon, luv.' Stabbed Man pulls his girlfriend out of line. 'Let's get to the hospital.'

'Oh, for fuck's sake,' whines Stabbed Man's Girlfriend. 'Trust you to get fucking Stanley-knifed on my one night out in fucking months.'

XXXIV

One hour later.

On the dance floor.

I've had five shots of vodka, two shots of Bacardi and a Southern Comfort.

I'm dancing alone.

Keith is in a dark corner snogging some bird he's picked up. I don't care. He can do what he likes. I just want to dance.

Above me, mirror-ball. I'm dripping with sweat.

Clothes stick to me. The boom-boom of the music cocoons me. Nothing else matters except the music. And the booze. And the sparkly lights. And the –

A surge of movement.

A scream!

Two girls fighting.

Clawing at each other. Kicking. There's blood on both their faces.

The crowd parts around them.

But the music continues.

The Fighting Girls are rolling on the ground now. Skirts up round their waists. Knickers showing.

Some blokes cheer.

And I watch as –

Claw! Scream! Mirror-ball! Kick! Blood! Rip! Boom-boom! Claw! Scratch! Tear! Cry! Blood! Dance! Scream!

– I can't think of anywhere else I'd rather be.

XXXV

Thirty minutes later.

I'm in the toilets.

Pissing in the urinal.

Then I hear –

In one of the cubicles. Panting. Groaning. I look under the door. Two pairs of feet. One male. One female. And then –

Knickers round ankles.

I hear the girl say, 'I'm . . . I'm having me period.'

The bloke says, 'You ain't now!'

A gasp from the girl and –

Plop!

Something has been thrown over the cubicle door.

It has landed at my feet like the guts of a bird.

It's a bloody tampon.

XXXVI

Ten minutes later.

Keith is on the dance floor. Smooching with yet another girl. He gives me a wink and beckons me over.

The three of us hug and dance.

We sway together.

Keith grabs my hand and puts it down to the girl's crotch.

It feels wet.

She looks at me and giggles.

Keith lifts the girl's dress, then thrusts my hand into her knickers.

I feel her wet pubic hair and slip a finger into her.

I do this for a while, then Keith joins in.

We both finger her.

I feel his finger against my finger.

I rest my head on his shoulder.

I smell his aftershave.

XXXVII

One hour later.

In the toilets.

Keith is hunched over a bog and he's vomiting.

I'm standing behind him, watching.

His shirt is stretched tight across his back. I see the caterpillar of his spine.

Slowly, I lift his shirt up.

Keith is still vomiting.

I push the shirt up . . . up . . .

The expanse of his back is like a new continent to explore.

'You okay, mate?' I ask.

Keith is retching too much to answer.

I close the cubicle door behind me.

I run my hands over Keith's back. It's so smooth and hard. Like peeled wood.

There's pornographic graffiti on the walls. Drawings of open cunts and ejaculating cocks.

I get a hard-on.

I unzip my trousers.

I get my cock out.

I rub my cock.

I touch Keith's back with my cock.

Keith is still vomiting.

I start to wank.

I rub . . .

Keith vomits . . .

I rub . . .

Keith vomits . . .

I spunk over Keith's back.

Keith finishes vomiting.

I put my cock away.

'Feeling better, mate?' I ask.

'Yeah,' he murmurs, getting to his feet. 'But . . . ' He reaches behind. 'Something dripped on me back.'

'Yeah,' I tell him. 'It's that pipe up there. It's leaking.'

XXXVIII

Later.

Dance floor.

Keith is snogging with yet another girl. I'm leaning against a wall. A couple are snogging beside me. When I glance down I see the girl unzip the bloke. She gets his cock out. She rubs it. And later –

XXXIX

A bloke is vomiting. It goes over two girls next to him. They scream and slap at him. As one girl strides off in a huff she slips in the puke. Falls on her arse. Everyone laughs. And later –

XL

A bloke starts taking his clothes off. A girl joins in. The bloke is fat and hairy. Hair all down his back. The girl flashes her arse. Bouncers step in and grab them. They are dragged half-naked, kicking and screaming, out of the disco. And later –

XLI

I'm dancing! A girl comes up and snogs me. Tongue in lung. She grabs me cock.
And later –

XLII

A fight! One bloke hits another. Blood! Screams! Others join in! Suddenly, the whole dance floor is erupting with –
Smashing glass!
Screams!
Keith puts his arm round my shoulder. 'Time to fuck off,' he says.
And later –

XLIII

We're in the car park.

    We're pissing against the wall.

    Keith aims his piss at me.

    I aim my piss at him.

    Piss goes over my shoes.

    Piss goes over his shoes.

    And later –

XLIV

We're weaving our way across the car park.

    Keith says, 'Look! There!'

    A couple are fucking in the back of a car. The windows are steamed up, but I can still make out –

    Heaving arse.

    A girl's tits.

    And hear them groaning.

    Keith and I creep forward.

    We watch.

    The girl looks over the bloke's shoulder and sees us.

    Keith and me go to scarper but –

    The girl smiles. She whispers something in the bloke's ear. He turns and looks at us.

    Keith and me go to scarper but –

    The bloke smiles. He reaches up and turns the car light on.

    The girl sucks the bloke's cock.

    Keith and me press our noses against the car window.

    We watch them suck and fuck.

    And, all the while, they're watching us . . . watching them . . . watching us . . . watching them . . .

    And later –

XLV

We're walking home.

Can't find a taxi for love nor money.

Keith takes something from his pocket. It's folded paper. About half the size of a packet of Rizlas.

'Look,' he says.

'What is it?'

He unfolds it to reveal white powder.

'Drug stuff?' I ask.

Keith nods.

I've never taken any drugs before. Nor has Keith. This is all new and thrilling.

'I bought it from one of the blokes in the cloakroom,' Keith says. 'It's speed or something. Ain't tried it yet.'

'Why not?'

'Kept bottling out.'

'Stupid cunt.'

'Yeah.'

'Shall we try it now?'

'But the night's fucking over.'

'So?'

'Well . . . you first, then.'

'What's it s'posed to do?'

'Keep you awake. Make you feel happy.'

'Do you . . . snort it?'

'Yeah. But the bloke I got it from said you can just dab it or something. You know? Lick your finger and stick it on and . . . you know.'

I lick, dab and lick.

Keith licks, dabs, licks.

It tastes bitter and I can't get rid of the taste.

'Ugh.'

'Ugh.'

We start walking towards the all-night garage down Mare Street so we can buy some lemonade or something to take away the taste and –

XLVI

– we're walking faster and faster and talking and –

XLVII

– we're running!

Running like we were born to run.

Running and talking and –

Jumping!

'Weeeee!'

'Weeeee!'

And laughing and running and talking and jumping.

My skin is tingling. My skull is buzzing. I can't stop talking. Keith is my best mate in the whole world. I tell him. I hold him. It's so important he knows. And Keith holds me and tells me the same sorts of things. We stand in a sodium-lit Mare Street and vow eternal friendship.

Everything is so fucking interesting all of a sudden.

Mare Street is more fascinating than the Amazon Jungle.

And later –

XLVIII

We're sitting on the kerb.

In the middle of the road is a tin can.

When a car drives over it –

Ka-ching!

'Yesss!' says Keith.

'Yesss!' I say.

This ka-chinging tin is the most engrossing phenomenon we've ever seen. We've been watching it for over an hour, debating if the approaching car will hit it, or miss it, or hit it, or miss –

'Ka-ching!'

'Yesss!'

'Yesss!'

And later –

XLIX

I'm saying to Keith, '– but soon me and Terry got bored with torturing insects and we moved on to bigger things like mice and stuff and one day we put our pocket money together and bought this hamster and we took it back to Terry's place and filled this big saucepan full of water and dropped the hamster in and then lit the gas underneath and watched as the water got hotter and hotter and the hamster was paddling around and around and then it was boiling and the hamster was splashing all over the place and then it went very still and we chucked it down the toilet and another time we bought this grass snake and sellotaped it to an electric bar on a heater and turned it on the snake started to twitch and the bar got red hot and then it started to really stink and this brown sort of liquid came out of the snake and the electric bar started to shoot out sparks and me and Terry screamed and turned it off and then we bought a baby rabbit –'

And later –

L

Keith is saying to me, '– and I thought that sexy bitch is gonna swallow my spunk if it kills me so I wanked non-stop for two days and collected all my spunk in an old film canister then when I had enough I put it in one of the squares of an ice-cube maker and froze it up and then I phoned and said, "Wanna come over to watch telly or something tonight Tracey?" and she said, "Yeah, all right, so long as your mum and dad are gonna be there, 'cos I don't want you groping me again," and I said, "Yeah, sure, Mum and Dad'll be there," and she came over and the four of us sat down and watched telly and after a while Mum says, "Get Tracey something to drink," and I said, "What d'you want, Trace?" and she said, "Coke," 'cos she always does and I said, "Ice?" and she said, "Yeah," 'cos she always does, and I pour her a glass of Coke and plop the spunk ice-cube in it and I give it to her and she drinks it all without batting an eyelid and I nearly cum in me pants watching her –'

LI

We're lying by the canal.

We're watching the sun coming up.

The speed is wearing off now.

I say softly, 'You know what I've got at home?'

'What?'

'Photographs of dead people.'

'Eh? What d'you mean?'

'Well . . . you remember that kid I used to be friends with at school? His family emigrated to Australia –'

'Simon Burnett?'

'Yeah. His dad was an undertaker.'

'I remember that, yeah.'

'Well . . . I used to take photos of the dead people. In their coffins. We'd creep down at night and – oh, I always touched them. I loved it! And I touched this kid's nipple once. And, another time, I kissed this old woman. Right on the lips –'

Keith stands up.

'Where're you going, mate?' I ask.

'Home,' Keith replies flatly. He glares at me a moment, then, 'You *are* a sicko sometimes, Phil. Really.'

Keith strides off.

I think about following him, then decide against it.

I watch Keith walk across the road.

'It's the truth!' I yell after him. 'I just told you the fucking truth, that's all.'

Keith doesn't look back.

I watch him walk down the road. I watch him till I can't see him any more.

Then I hear something splash in the canal. I look round but –

Whatever it was has disappeared.

All that's left are ripples.

LII

I'm eighteen.

I'm so drunk . . . Where am I? A pub somewhere . . . What pub? Looks like The Seabright. No, no, can't be! That's where I started. Hours ago. Alone. I went there . . . Had a few Southern Comforts and lemonade. Then – alone – made my way to . . . The Hackney Carriage. Few more Southern Comforts. Then I went to . . . The Queen's! That's right! And then after that . . . fuck knows! All I'm sure of is . . . I'm in this place! Red velvet

wallpaper . . . mirror-ball . . . lots of smoke – what's
happening now?

Someone's walked onto the little makeshift stage. He's
about nineteen years old. He's wearing a sequinned
jacket . . . Oh, no! Not pub entertainment! Some corny
magician or crooner . . . I don't want to be entertained.
I just want to get totally rat-arsed. I've had one of my
dark days. I woke up depressed and it's just got worse
and worse. This afternoon I felt so skinned a screeching
car tyre made me weep. The only cure is . . . this! A
million Southern Comforts and eventual oblivion.

Wait a minute!

Sequin Jacket is not a magician.

He's not a crooner either . . .

He's opening a matchbox . . .

Taking something out.

What is it?

A slug!

The largest, greenest, sluggiest slug I've ever seen.

Sequin Jacket is licking it . . . The audience is backing
away . . . I move closer . . . Sequin Jacket opens his
mouth . . . Sequin Jacket puts the slug inside . . . Sequin
Jacket eats it!

The audience goes, 'Ughh!'

I move closer.

Sequin Jacket opens another box.

A worm!

Sequin Jacket picks it up . . .

Sequin Jacket opens his mouth . . .

Sequin Jacket eats the worm . . .

The audience goes, 'Ughh!'

I move closer.

And, as I watch, my dark mood disperses. Watching
Sequin Jacket is a more delightful oblivion than a vat full
of Southern Comfort.

Beetles!
'Ughh!'
I move closer.
Spider!
'Ughh!'
Closer.

LIII

'Hello? Phil? Me. Dave. Sorry for ringing so late. Tell
your mum I'm sorry. Weren't asleep, were you? Oh, shit,
that's right. You're starting college tomorrow. But I had
to ring. I've just had a phone call from Debbie. Yeah,
Rick's Debbie. Listen, Phil, you best sit down . . . You
know that party we were supposed to go to last night?
That's right. The one in Stepney. Well, Rick went and –
no, no, don't interrupt. Listen, mate, listen! Rick and
Debbie went. And . . . well, on the way home they were
walking down Mile End Road when . . . this car pulls
up. Four guys get out. Rick and Debbie don't know these
guys from Adam. And . . . well, these guys grab hold of
Rick and start beating him up. No reason. Just for the
fun of it. And . . . one bloke has got a knife, right. And –
anyway – Rick gets stabbed. Seven fucking times. These
cunts are laughing and laughing. Then they jump in their
fucking car and drive away. And Rick's on the pavement.
And he's covered in blood. Debbie's fucking panicking.
She don't know what to fucking do. Poor cow. Cars
are driving by. Does anyone stop? Course not! No one
gives a fuck! Bastards! Anyway, Debbie – she has to
leave Rick where he is. Go and find a call-box. Phone for
an ambulance. Fucking shit, right? And . . . well, when
she gets back there's even more blood. That's all she kept
saying to me, "There was so much blood." And . . .

and . . . anyway, they get Rick to fucking hospital. And . . .
they open up Rick's chest. And his lung has been
punctured or something. And . . . they operate on him
all night. He's in intensive care now. No one knows if
he's going to make it or not – Why am I laughing? Fuck!
You too! Stop it, Phil! Fuck! We mustn't laugh! Fuck!
Mustn't laugh!'

LIV

'Hello, Phil. Dave. Just wondering if you're OK. I mean,
you left the drinks thing after the funeral so early. What
d'you call that anyway? The drinks and sandwiches part?
Is it a wake? No, no, don't blame you for pissing off
at all, old son. Totally depressing. Rick's mum kept the
fucking waterworks going all night. Poor old cow . . .
Listen, Phil. Guess what? You know I've fancied Debbie
for years. Since we were fourteen. Anyway, after the
bevvy and sarnies I offered to drive her home. Everyone
else was legless and she was in no fit state for the bus.
So . . . there we are. In the car. And she's blubbering and
blubbering. Talking about Rick and all that. And I'm
saying, "Yeah, yeah, I understand, he was my best mate,
don't forget." Even though he ain't. Wasn't. Anyway –
to cut a long story short – I park the car down a back
street and put my arm round her and . . . well, fuck me
if I don't get a hard-on! I think to myself, This is your
chance, old son. While she's all weak and wobbly. So
I start a little bit of snogging and groping. She keeps
bursting into tears in my face. And I'm loving it, ain't I?
And . . . well, I fuck her. There. In the car. With her
crying and saying Rick's name over and over again. And
I tell you this – horniest fuck of my life. No bullshit.
Horny as fucking hell.'

LV

I'm twenty-five years old. How did that happen? I hate it!
I'm not meant to be this old. I'm meant to be a nineteen.
I want people to think me nineteen. I want to be friends
with people who are nineteen. I want to go to places
for people who are nineteen. I don't want to be this age.
When I look at my reflection I see things changing.
Look! A grey hair! Disgusting! I'll have to dye it. And
I'm sure my eyes are getting smaller. They're definitely
losing their sparkle. Pores in my skin getting larger. I'm
putting on weight. It's all happening too quickly. Like a
horror film. Like a vampire in sunlight. The worst thing
is . . . having sex with people my own age. What a
revolting prospect! I want to have sex with nineteen-
year-olds. Youth! But now – nineteen-year-olds see me
as ancient. I've become something separate from them.
I can't laugh and flirt with them and go to their places.
I hate it! Also, it's not safe to have sex with people my
age. The older someone is, the more experience they've
had. And more experience means infection. The younger
they are, the safer their –

LVI

– blood. Every time I have sex that's all I think of.
Blood. Other people's blood. What if their gums start
bleeding? What if my nails graze them? What if my cock
tears them . . . ? What's that taste in my mouth? Is it
blood? – Ahhh! That hurt! Am I bleeding? Are you
bleeding? Are we bleeding? Is that blood? Whose blood
is that? How many people have you made bleed? How
much blood has there been in your life? Is there blood
on your hands? Oh, let's talk about blood. If you talk

about yours, I'll talk about mine. Is that blood in your pocket or are you just pleased to see me? Yes, blood is the subject. Blood! Blood! Blood!

LVII

Saturday morning.

I'm sitting on the top deck of a bus. I'm on my way to see my friend, Dominic. His mum rang last night and asked me to visit. 'He's scaring me, Phil,' she said. 'I don't know why he does . . . what he does. Oh, please have a chat with him. He trusts you.'

Ouch! What's that?

Something just hit my head!

An empty Coke can!

I look round. Three girls are sitting a few seats behind. They're the only other people up here, so it must have been them.

And yet –

They're so young. Only nine or ten years. And they look so harmless and innocent.

I scowl at them, turn to the front again and –

Crack!

Another tin can hits my head!

I glare at the girls.

They're giggling now.

'Stop it!' I tell them.

'Fuck off!'

'Fuck off!'

'Fuck off!'

One of them throws something else. I'm not even sure what it is. But it hits my forehead.

I jump to my feet. 'I told you to stop –'

'Wanna fight?'

'Fucking kill ya!'

'Kick ya teeth in!'

I'm so angry I want to smash their pretty young faces against the windows until bone and glass crack. But . . . how can I? They're just little girls. Children. No one would believe that –

They're walking towards me.

I back away. 'Leave me alone –'

'You prick!'

'You bastard!'

'You shit!'

One girls kicks me. The other spits at my face. The third is laughing too much to do anything.

I try to push them away.

'Prick!'

'Bastard!'

'Shit!'

All three of them are kicking me now. Really hard. I feel blood trickling down my shin –

'Hey! Cut it out, you lot!'

It's the bus conductor.

'Our stop anyway!' cries one of the girls.

And the three of them rush off.

'Did . . . did you see that?' I stammer, breathlessly. 'They . . . they really wanted to . . . to hurt me. They . . . they . . .'

But the conductor is chuckling and walking downstairs. 'Kids, eh?' he says.

LVIII

Saturday afternoon.

I'm sitting in Dominic's mum's living-room. Dominic's mum is bathing the graze on my forehead. Dominic's gran is sitting in an armchair, watching.

'I don't know what's happening to the world any more,' says Dominic's mum. 'Little girls doing this! Good Lord! They're getting younger and younger. I see them from the window, you know. In the car park opposite. Doing all their drug stuff. Buying and selling. I tell you, some of them are just babies. In the morning, there's needles all over the bloody place. Hundreds of them. They go crunch, crunch, crunch when you walk over them. That person Dominic gets all his drugs from – oh, yes, I've seen him. He's come round here. Bold as brass. Flash car. Gold rings. Tattoo all up his arm. Can't be any more than seventeen. Good Lord! When I was that age two Babychams were my limit. They were all I could afford, for one thing. But now . . . these dealers throw money round like there's no tomorrow. All they're worried about is snazzy clothes.'

'Snazzy!' says Dominic's gran. 'They don't know the meaning of the word. In my day gangsters *really* knew how to dress. They were smart. And polite. I tell you something else for nothing. They were gangsters for a reason. They wanted to better themselves. They wanted to know posh people. Get into posh places. They wanted to improve their lives. But crooks these days . . . it's all drugs and smashing people's faces in. They talk like commoners. They're nothing. And they do terrible things.'

'But criminals did terrible things in your day too,' I tell her. 'They were very violent –'

'They might have been!' snaps Dominic's gran. 'But at least they wore smart suits.'

LIX

A bedroom in a council flat in Bethnal Green, the East End of London. Early evening. Summer's sunlight can be detected behind the pulled curtains. Magazines are strewn across the floor. A plate of half-eaten food on the sideboard. Piles of records and paperbacks. Posters of science-fiction films across the walls. Against one wall is an unmade bed. On this bed is Dominic.

Dominic is in his late twenties. He is wearing a T-shirt and boxer shorts. His hair is shaven at the sides, long on top, like a horse's mane.

I am sitting on a pile of cushions next to the bed.

Dominic says, 'So you're my Rosencrantz and Guildenstern all rolled into one, eh? Sent by Mum to check on her crazy offspring.'

'You ain't crazy.'

'*She* thinks I am. Pops her head round the door every ten minutes to make sure I ain't cut me throat.'

'She's worried.'

'I ain't trying to kill myself, Phil. You know that. I just like . . . hurting myself. When I did this –' He indicates the bandages on his left arm '– it was such a fucking buzz, man. Really. I grabbed the scissors. Stuck them in here –' Touches upper arm '– and dragged them down to here.' Touches wrist. 'You could hear the fucking skin tearing. And the blood. Better than any drug, I tell you. Seventy-three fucking stitches. Due out in two days.' He gives me a sly smile. 'Might rip them out before then and start all over again.'

A rap at the door.

His mum pops her head in. 'You want anything, luv?'

'Yeah. Some razor blades and a noose.'

'Oh, don't, Dom.' She starts weeping. 'Please.'

Dominic jumps off the bed. 'Come on,' he says to me. 'Let's get out of Elsinore.'

LX

Ten minutes later.

We're walking through the estate.

It's very dark and strangely quiet.

Dominic says, 'Remember when we first met. That day in the coffee bar at St Martin's. I couldn't believe there was anyone else from East London who liked painting and stuff. Let alone managed to get into Art School. I always thought I was the only one.'

'Me too.'

'D'you ever wonder what it might've been like if we'd met before? You know? When we were kids. Toddlers. How different things would've been. If we'd grown up with someone to talk to about all the stuff in our heads, wouldn't that have been wicked, eh?'

'Yeah.'

LXI

Five minutes later.

We stroll into an empty playground.

We sit on the swings.

Dominic says, 'You were the only one who liked my stuff, you know. At the beginning. Those paintings I did using my own blood and spunk. Everyone thought they were just shock tactics.'

'I love shock tactics.'

'Long live the ghost train, right?'

'Long live the ghost train.'

'Make 'em scream!'

'Make 'em dream!'

'You know, Phil, I've been thinking and . . . well, you do a painting – or a novel, anything – and it's like . . . planting a tree. The tree grows. It bears fruit. Oh, sure you try to prune it and water it properly but, in the end, it's just . . . a particular kind of tree that bears a particular kind of fruit. Fuck messages. Fuck morals. Fuck meanings. And people either like the fruit or they don't.'

LXII

Two minutes later.

We're sitting on the roundabout.

Dominic says, 'When I sliced my arm open . . . I rushed out of the flat. I came here. There's still blood on the ground if you look. And on this roundabout. Here – look! See? The kids love it. Anyway . . . I came here. Buzzing with pain. High. Really high. And I looked up. Like when I was a kid. Just like I'm doing now. And then . . . I saw it.'

'Saw what?'

'I thought it was a hole in space at first. Because that's what it looked like. All the stars had disappeared, you see. But then . . . then I realised. It wasn't a hole. It was an object. A gleaming, dark, silent object. Just floating up there. And . . . and it was huge. The size of . . . oh, three or four tower blocks. And . . . jet black and gleaming. And I knew that this was its only purpose. Its sole function. To be jet black and gleaming. And . . . I felt so peaceful looking at it. Watching this . . . gleaming dark.'

THE PITCHFORK DISNEY

For Joe Hutton –
who spits fire

Fears are more personal than we had guessed –
We only need ourselves: time does the rest.
Elizabeth Jennings

Extreme terror gives us back the gestures of our
childhood.
Chazal

Through indiscriminate suffering men know
fear and fear is the most divine emotion. It is the
stories for altars and the beginning of wisdom.
Half-gods are worshipped in wine and flowers.
Real gods require blood.
Zora Neale Hurston

Characters

Presley Stray
Haley Stray
Cosmo Disney
Pitchfork Cavalier

The Pitchfork Disney was premièred at the Bush Theatre, London, on 2 January 1991, with the following cast:

Presley Stray Rupert Graves
Haley Stray Tilly Vosburgh
Cosmo Disney Dominic Keating
Pitchfork Cavalier Stuart Raynor

Directed by Matthew Lloyd
Décor Moggie Douglas
Lighting Danielle Bisson
Music Nick Bicat

*Night. A dimly lit room in the East End of London:
front door with many bolts, black overcoat hanging on
hook, chest of drawers, table, two hardbacked chairs,
two armchairs, electric bar fire in front of one armchair,
doorway leading to tiny kitchen (where a fridge is
visible). Everything old and colourless.*

*Presley Stray, twenty-eight years old, is standing by the
window. He is dressed in a black T-shirt and jeans. He is
unshaven, hair unevenly cut very short, skin pale, dark
rings beneath bloodshot eyes. He is staring into the
darkness outside.*

*Haley Stray, his twenty-eight-year-old sister, is sitting at
the table. She is wearing a black T-shirt and jeans. Her
hair is longer than her brother's, but still unevenly cut,
and she's got the same complexion. She is fiddling with
a shiny-red piece of chocolate wrapping paper.*

Sounds of dogs howling outside.

Haley flinches, looks at Presley anxiously.
  Presley looks at her.

The dogs continue howling.
  Pause.

Sound of dogs fades.

Presley looks out of window.
  Haley continues to look anxious.

Haley Describe it.

Presley Again?

Haley Once more.

Presley You said that last time.

Haley Did I? Don't remember.

Presley You know your trouble? You break your promises. You say one thing but you mean another. You don't play fair. Sometimes I think you ain't nothing but a –

Haley What?

Presley Oh, nothing.

Haley Go on. Say it.

Presley A cheat.

Haley Don't call me that. It's not fair. Not after what happened this morning.

Presley What d'you mean?

Haley With the shopping.

Presley What about it?

Haley The chocolate, Presley. I'm talking about the chocolate. You bought fruit and nut.

Presley So?

Haley You know I don't like fruit and nut. You know it makes me sick. The nut . . . it gets caught between my teeth. The raisins . . . they . . .

Presley What?

Haley Taste like bits of skin.

Presley How d'you know what skin tastes like?

Haley Can use my imagination.

Presley Well, you used to like fruit and nut.

Haley Never. *You* like fruit and nut. *My* favourite is orange chocolate.

Slight pause.

Presley I didn't just buy fruit and nut. I bought other things as well.

Haley What other things?

Presley Lots of things.

Haley Didn't tell me.

Presley Did, Haley.

Haley Must have forgotten. Where are they?

Presley In the drawer.

Haley goes to drawer in sideboard. She opens it, discovers many bars of different chocolate. Most is in shiny wrapping paper.

Haley Oh, Presley. You did. You *really* did . . . I can see orange chocolate.

Takes chocolate to table.

Come and eat, Presley.

Presley No thanks.

Haley You're sulking now.

Presley You shouldn't accuse me of just buying fruit and nut.

Haley I'm sorry. It's just that I saw you eating a bar earlier and I . . . well, I assumed that's all there was. I can see now . . . there's a big selection . . . Come on.

Waves bar temptingly in the air.

Fruit and nut . . . Fruit and nut . . .

Presley rushes to table. They sit and begin to eat.

Presley There's more chocolate than ever in the shops now. You go in – it sparkles like treasure. Flaky chocolate, mint chocolate, crispy chocolate –

Haley Bubbly chocolate –

Presley Wafer chocolate –

Haley Chocolate with cream in –

Presley Chocolate with nuts in –

Haley Which I don't like!

Presley Which you don't like. All sorts of chocolate in all sorts of paper.

Haley is sorting through the pile for another bar of orange chocolate.

Haley Well, that's typical!

Presley What?

Haley You bought . . . one, two, three, four, five, plus the one you're eating, plus the one this morning, that's seven bars of fruit and nut and only one bar of orange.

Slight pause.

Presley I must have got carried away.

Haley This is just like you, Presley. Sometimes you're so –

Presley What?

Haley Oh, nothing.

Presley Go on. Say it.

Haley Selfish.

Presley Don't call me that. It's not fair. Not after what *you* did this morning.

Haley What did I do?

Presley About going out to get the shopping in the first place.

Haley So?

Presley It was *your* turn.

Haley Was not.

Presley Was!

Haley Wasn't!

Presley Was!

Haley Wasn't!

Presley Was! Was! Was!

Haley How? How was it my turn?

Presley I went yesterday.

Haley You didn't.

Presley Did. You know I did. I bought the milk. And the bread. They were in a brown paper bag. I put them on the table. You were sitting where you're sitting now. You said, 'Didn't you buy any biscuits?' And I said, 'Yes.' I gave them to you. They were in a blue packet. I made you a cup of tea. You dunked the biscuits. Afterwards I put what was left of the biscuits in the fridge.

Haley Biscuits? In the fridge?

Presley Yes.

Haley In a blue packet?

Presley Yes.

Haley A blue packet with yellow and red stripes?

Presley Yes.

Haley That means they're orange chocolate biscuits.

Presley I know.

Haley Well, why didn't you tell me? I've felt like a biscuit all day.

Presley Surely you saw me put them in the fridge.

Haley I forgot. You know I need reminding. If you make me a cup of tea and don't offer me a biscuit, then I assume all the biscuits have gone. I don't think you're hiding them from me.

Presley I wasn't!

Haley You were! You were going to wait for me to take my tablet, then eat them all yourself.

Presley But I don't even like the biscuits. I got them for you. You're just trying to change the subject.

Haley . . . From what?

Presley From why you said it wasn't your turn to get the shopping when you know full well it was.

Slight pause.

Haley Don't blame me. You . . . you remember what happened last time I went to the shops.

Presley What?

Haley Oh . . . it was terrible.

Presley What?

Slight pause.

Come on!

Haley I was so scared. I came back crying and shaking.
My clothes were torn and wet. There was blood on my
legs. You wiped it away with a tissue. I was crying so
much I couldn't breathe properly. I was hysterical. You
remember that, Presley?

Presley I . . . might do.

Haley You were so nice. You put your arms round me.
And I told you what happened.

Presley Tell me again. Go on. If it's good enough . . . I'll
do all the shopping in future.

Slight pause.

Haley When I got to the end of the street a . . . a pack
of dogs appeared. Seven of them. Big, filthy dogs. With
maggots in their fur. Foam on their lips. Eyes like clots
of blood.

Presley Good, good.

Haley One dog started to sniff me. Its nose was like
an ice cube between my legs. Then it started to growl.
Lips pulled back over yellow teeth. It started to chase me.
I was running. Running and screaming. The other dogs
chased me as well. All of them howling and snarling like
wolves. They chased me over the waste ground. I fell.
Fell into a pile of tin cans. There was a dead cat. My
hand went into its stomach. All mushy like rotten fruit.
I was screaming. Screaming so loud my throat tasted like
blood. One of the dogs bit my coat. I pulled it away. The
coat ripped. I ran and ran. All I could hear was snarling
and growling and the sound of my own heart. I ran
out of the waste ground. Through the old car park and
into the derelict church. Still the dogs chased me. There
I was, standing at the altar, with seven rabid animals
coming down the aisles towards me. I picked up some

old Bibles and threw them. Did no good. The dogs ripped the Bibles to pieces. I was so afraid. And the dogs – they could smell it. My fear. They were attracted by it. They came closer and closer and closer. I could feel their breath against my skin. Hot and reeking of vomit. I backed away. Stumbled up some steps. I wanted to pray. But I couldn't. I knew that if I could pray or sing a hymn, then the dogs would leave me alone. But all I could do was scream. Then one of the dogs made a lunge for me. I jumped up. Reached above me. Caught hold of something. It was smooth. Cool. Solid. I started to climb. Like climbing a tree. I was halfway up before I realised I was climbing the marble crucifix and my chest was pressed against the chest of Christ. It felt so comforting and safe. Then a dog bit at my feet. Pulled my shoe off. My toes were bleeding. A drop of blood landed in the open mouth of the dog. It went berserk. It started to climb the crucifix. I scarpered higher. Wrapped my legs round the waist of our Saviour. Clung onto the crown of thorns for all I was worth. Then the base of the crucifix started to crumble. It rocked from side to side. Any minute it might fall and send me into the pack of dogs. Like a Christian to the hungry lions. I was so scared. I kissed the lips of Christ. I said, 'Save me! Don't let the crucifix fall!' But the crucifix fell just the same. Crashed to the floor. The dogs nibbled at my bloodied fingers. I'm going to be eaten alive, I thought. Eaten by savage dogs. I screamed, 'Help me! Help me!' And then . . . gunshots! I flinch at every one. Look round. The seven dogs are dead. Blood oozing from holes in their skulls. I feel sick. A priest approaches me. He's holding a rifle. He asks if I'm all right. I tell him I am. He says, 'Did you come for confession?' And I say, 'Yes,' because I think that's what he wants to hear and I owe him something for saving my life. So I go into confession with him and he asks me what I've done wrong. I tell

him I can't think of anything. He says, 'Don't be stupid.
No one's perfect.' I know he's right. I know there's
something I've done. Something that made me a naughty
girl once. But I can't think of what it is. I tell him I can't
think of anything. He tells me to think harder. I can feel
him getting angry and frustrated. He wants to forgive me
but I'm not giving him the chance. Finally I say, 'I kissed
the lips of Christ and they tasted of chocolate.' He calls
me a sinner and says I must repent. I ask him if I can be
forgiven and he says, 'No! Your sins are too big.' I'm
crying when I leave the church. Hysterical. Hysterical.

Pause.

Presley You'll never have to go shopping again.

Haley Promise?

Presley Promise.

Haley Cross your heart?

Presley Cross my heart.

Haley And hope to die?

Presley Certainly.

Haley Say it.

Presley Hope to die.

Haley Thank you, Presley. You don't know what that
means to me. Some days I sit in dread, just waiting for
the moment I'll have to face things outside.

Presley Well, you won't have to any more. I'll get all the
shopping in future.

Haley Perhaps we should put it in writing.

Presley Why?

Haley In case you forget.

Presley I won't.

Haley You might.

Presley This is just like you, Haley. Sometimes you're so –

Haley What?

Presley Oh, nothing.

Haley Go on. Say it.

Presley Suspicious.

Haley Don't call me that. It's not fair.

Slight pause.

Not after what *you* did the other day.

Presley What did I do?

Haley Accused me of taking an extra tablet when I didn't.

Presley Haley, there are only two of us here. Just you and me. There were seven tablets in the bottle. I counted them. The next morning there were six. If I didn't take an extra one, where did it go?

Haley Well, I didn't take it.

Presley Not knowingly.

Haley What's that supposed to mean?

Presley You could have taken it when you were sleep-walking.

Haley I don't do that any more.

Presley You do. I watch you. You sleepwalk. And talk.

Haley Talk? What do I say?

Presley Lots of things.

Haley Like what?

Presley Don't remember.

Haley That's because I don't do it.

Presley You *do*!

Haley Then give me a for-instance.

Presley For instance . . . Well, the last time you were calling 'Mummy! Daddy!' I think you were lost in the zoo again.

Haley Oh, that was a terrible day, Presley. How old were we?

Presley Six.

Haley There were snakes. And lizards. And all kinds of crawly things. It was dark. I was crying, 'Mummy! Daddy . . .! I'm lost . . . I'm so scared!'

Presley That's exactly what you were doing the other night. Standing in the middle of the room and crying over and over again. 'I'm so scared . . . I'm so scared.'

Slight pause.

Haley Well, I don't care what you say. I still think you took the tablet.

Presley Why would I do that?

Haley Because of your nightmare. You want to sleep so deep you don't have it.

Presley The nightmare comes no matter how many tablets I take.

Slight pause.

Anyway, the nightmare don't scare me any more.

Haley Oh, Presley.

Presley What?

Haley Sometimes you're such a –

Presley What?

Haley Oh, nothing.

Presley Say it.

Slight pause.

Say it!

Haley Liar!

Presley Haley!

Haley It's true. To sit there and tell me you're not scared is just ridiculous. *I* know it! *You* know it!

Pause.

Presley I . . . I had the nightmare last night.

Haley Was it . . . the same?

Presley Oh, yeah. Everything. It never changes. I woke up crying and . . . I'd bitten my mouth. My spit was all red.

Haley Did it give you an ulcer?

Presley Yeah.

Haley Show me.

Presley pulls down his bottom lip.
Haley looks at ulcer.

Haley It's like a tiny yellow crater.

Presley Tiny? Feels huge.

Haley Is it sore?

Presley A bit.

Haley Is talking difficult?

Presley Not really.

Haley Then will you describe it? Just once more. Then I'll take my tablet. I promise, Presley. Cross my heart.

Pause.

Presley goes to the window.

Presley Where shall I begin?

Haley The sky.

Presley It's black. A sheet of dark cloud obscures everything. No heaven visible. No stars, no moon, no sun. Nothing.

Haley Is it snowing?

Presley Slightly.

Haley Is it true, Presley, that no two snowflakes are the same? Remember our schoolteacher showed us this photograph of a snowflake enlarged a million times. It was like a stained-glass window. So delicate. She said, 'No matter how much it snows, even if it snows from now until the end of time, every snowflake will be unique.' What a miracle!

Presley It's not a miracle.

Haley . . . No?

Presley It's just what happens after an apocalypse. That's all.

Slight pause.

You want to hear about the street or not?

Haley Course I do! The street. Describe the street, Presley.

Presley Well . . . you remember the corner shop? The one where we got all our shopping. Where the shopkeeper called Mummy 'Mrs Stray' and always asked how Daddy was.

Haley The shop where we bought our sweets?

Presley The very same.

Haley Remember.

Presley It's gone.

Haley Totally?

Presley Utterly. Nothing left but scorched wood and blistered glass. Razed to the ground. And the shopkeeper –

Haley Who said, 'Hello, Mrs Stray. How's Mr Stray?'

Presley The very same. He's gone as well.

Haley Totally?

Presley Utterly. Burnt to nothing. Incinerated. One flash of light and – vooosh!

Haley But . . . he was such a nice man.

Presley One nice man amongst millions.

Haley Billions.

Presley Is the world worth saving for one nice man?

Haley Certainly not.

Presley Exactly.

Haley And the rest of the street? Describe the rest.

Presley The same as the shop. Just burnt and blistered. The whole world is a wasteland. Black sky. Black earth.

Black nothing. Some areas are still smouldering, cooled only by the gentle snowfall.

Haley It sounds beautiful.

Presley It has a certain beauty.

Haley But, Presley, if everything has gone . . . that means . . . we're the only ones left.

Presley That's right.

Haley And this house is the only house standing.

Presley That's right.

Haley Standing like a dark tower in a wasteland.

Presley Oh, well done, Haley. That's exactly what it looks like. We'll have to remember that.

Slight pause.

Haley But why did we survive, Presley? Why did we survive the end of it all?

Presley Because we were good children, that's why. What did Daddy always say to you?

Haley 'What a good girl you are.'

Presley And what did Mummy always say to me?

Haley 'What a good boy you are.'

Presley That's right. So we were good children and never made a noise and always ate our vegetables and said please and thank you and washed our hands before eating and after going to the toilet and always went to bed when we were told to.

Haley And Mummy and Daddy said we were the best children in the world.

Presley That's right. We were never naughty.

Haley Never.

Pause.

Except . . . that time.

Presley That time?

Haley When I wandered off and got lost in the zoo.

Presley It was only once, Haley.

Slight pause.

Haley Did you ever do anything naughty?

Presley Where'd that question come from?

Haley Just thought of it – vooosh!

Presley You're a real live wire tonight.

Haley Well, did you?

Presley What?

Haley Do anything naughty?

Presley No.

Haley Not once?

Presley No.

Haley You must have done. I remember Mum hitting you. She slapped your legs till they were bright red.

Slight pause.

You cried.

Presley How old were we?

Haley About ten.

Slight pause.

Oh, come on. A naughty thing. Please!

Slight pause.

Presley I saved my pocket money for three weeks. I didn't buy anything. No comics, no crisps, no sweets. I went to a pet shop and bought this tiny green snake instead. A grass snake they called it. When I got home I played with the snake. It felt warm and soft. I was scared but I still had to hold it. I liked the way it wrapped itself round my fingers like an electric shoelace. And then . . . then I realised. I could never keep it. Not as a pet. Where would it sleep? What would it eat? Where would it go when I went to school? It was a stupid thing to buy. So I had to get rid of it. But how? All sorts of things occurred to me. Flush it down the toilet, bury it, throw it from a tower block. But all the while another thought was taking shape. A thought so wonderful it seemed the only thing to do. So I got a frying pan and put it on the gas stove. I put a bit of butter in the pan and turned the gas up full. The fat started to crackle and smoke. I dropped the snake into the frying pan. It span round and round and its skin burst open like the skin of a sausage. It took ages to die. Its tiny mouth opened and closed and its black eyes exploded. Oh, it was wonderful to watch. All that burning and scalding and peeling. I got a fork and stuck the prongs into its skin. Boiling black blood bubbled out of the holes. When the snake was dead I put it on a plate. I cut the snake into bite size pieces. I tasted it. Like greasy chicken. I ate it all and licked the plate afterwards. When Mum got home she saw I'd been cooking and hit me. She didn't know anything about the snake. All she was worried about was the scorched patch on the frying pan. She said, 'I'll have to buy a new one now.' But she never did.

27

Rushes to the kitchen and gets scorched frying pan.

Look!

Haley Oh, take it away. Makes me feel sick.

Slight pause.

How could you eat a snake?

Presley It seemed inevitable somehow.

Slight pause.

You want those biscuits now?

Haley You see what I'm like? I forget everything. Even biscuits. Yes, Presley. Please. I'll have the biscuits now.

Presley gets the biscuits from fridge. He hands them to Haley.

Haley Sometimes I wake up and I have such a craving in my mouth.

Presley I know . . .

Haley (*with Presley*) Chocolate!

Presley (*with Haley*) Chocolate!

Haley Sometimes I dream that everything is made out of chocolate. I dream I live in a chocolate house and when I get hungry I just eat the walls. Or the floor. Or the tables. Because everything's chocolate. I even dreamt I ate a man made of chocolate. Ate every little bit till there was nothing left but his clothes. His clothes were shiny red chocolate paper. They say that eating chocolate gives you the same feeling as falling in love. It releases the same chemicals into the bloodstream. No wonder people like falling in love. What d'you think falling in love's like, Presley?

Presley Scary.

Haley More scary than being lost?

Presley About the same.

Haley Yeah. About the same.

Presley hears something outside. A faint, half-human, half-animal cry.

Haley What's wrong?

Presley I . . . I heard something.

Haley Where?

Presley In the street.

Haley What?

Presley Something . . . different.

Looks out of the window.

Haley What is it?

Presley A man . . . He's clutching his stomach.

Haley Is he ill?

Presley I think so. He's . . . he's got a friend with him. The friend's helping him sit on the kerb.

Haley You think he's drunk?

Presley Might be.

Haley Come away. They might see you.

Presley They won't.

Haley They might. You remember what happened last time. Those boys threw things at the window. We hid under the table.

Presley He *is* ill, Haley. He's rocking backwards and forwards. Must be in pain. His friend's just watching.

Haley What does he look like?

Presley What one?

Haley The one sitting down. The sick one. Would you call him good-looking?

Presley Yeah.

Haley Attractive?

Presley Yeah.

Haley And the other one. The one who's just watching.

Presley I . . . I can't tell. He looks . . . foreign.

Haley A foreigner! Oh, come away, Presley. You know what Mum and Dad said about foreigners. They're dangerous, Presley. Dangerous and different. They beat up women and abuse children. They don't do things the way we do. They hate us. They'd kill us all if they had the chance.

Presley Calm down, Haley.

Haley Is the door bolted?

Presley Yes.

Haley All the bolts?

Presley Every one.

Haley And the chain?

Presley The chain's on. We're perfectly safe.

Haley The door can still be knocked down. They'll see you looking at them. They'll take an instant dislike to you the way people do. They'll break the door down and –

Presley I'll get your tablet!

Haley No!

Presley You promised to take one.

Haley Not now.

Presley goes to chest of drawers, opens a drawer and removes a bottle of tablets. He shakes a tablet into his hand. Puts bottle on table.

Haley They'll hurt me when I'm asleep. Do terrible things to me. With razor blades and broken glass. They'll kiss me and cut me.

Presley grabs hold of Haley.

Presley Come on.

Haley No! Don't! I'm not playing games now. I'm not –

Presley forces Haley's mouth open and throws a few tablets inside. He closes her mouth, puts hand over it. He pinches her nose with his other hand.

Haley stares.

Presley Swallow.

Slight pause.

Swallow.

Haley swallows.

Presley Good girl.

Sits her down, tucks blankets round her.

There. Now just calm down. Nothing terrible's going to happen.

Goes back to window.

Pause.

Haley What's . . . what's going on now?

Presley He's moving off – the foreign-looking one. He's left the other one – the good-looking one – in the gutter.

Haley What's he doing in the gutter?

Presley Still rocking backwards and forwards. He must have such a bad stomach ache. He can't move with the agony.

Haley Just . . . just come away from the window. That's all I ask. It might develop into something nasty. You know how easily horrible things happen. Don't you? Eh? The police will come and ask questions. They'll suspect you're holding something back and lock you up.

Presley Don't work yourself into a state. The tablet will take effect soon.

Haley They'll take you from me. I'll be all alone. I'll have to get the shopping and talk to the postman and let the gas man in and pay electric bills.

Presley I'll get you the dummy. You want the dummy?

Haley I'll have to take the rubbish out.

Presley goes over to the drawer where he got the tablets and starts searching.

Haley I'll have to sweep the pavement and say good morning to the neighbours –

Presley Where's Mum and Dad's medicine, Haley?

Looks elsewhere.

Where's the bloody dummy and medicine?

Haley I'll have to go to the hairdresser's and get my hair cut. I'll have to tip the girl who washes my hair. I'll have to buy all my own chocolate. I'll buy seven bars and only have enough for six. I'll be accused of shoplifting. I'll have to get on a bus and pay my fare. I'll miss my stop . . .

Presley finds dummy and medicine in fridge.

Presley What's it doing in here? Eh? Did you bloody put it in here?

Haley I'll have to stand behind people in queues. People will push and shove and tell me I'm in the way . . .

Presley has opened the medicine. He dips the dummy into bottle, coating the teat with liquid. He puts bottle on table and takes dummy to Haley.

Presley touches dummy to Haley's lips.

Presley Suck!

Haley No.

Presley Suck!

Haley Don't make me.

Presley Suck! Suck! Suck! Suck! Suck!

Forces dummy into her mouth.

Suck!

Slight pause.

Suck!

Haley begins to suck.

Presley Harder.

Haley sucks harder.
Slight pause.

33

Presley You're a good girl, Haley. You know that?

Goes back to window.

Haley Don't think it matters if I'm good or not. Not when so much in life can explode. So many things can burn us up through no fault of our own. There's nothing we can do to save ourselves. That's what scares me.

Presley returns to her and they embrace.

Presley Shall I describe it again?

Haley sleepily nods.

Presley The sky is black. A sheet of dark cloud obscures everything. No heaven visible. No stars, no moon. Nothing. And the corner shop has gone. Nothing left except scorched wood and blistered glass. And the shopkeeper's gone as well. Incinerated. One flash of light and he was turned into an X-ray and then he didn't exist any more.

Haley Vooosh!

Presley Very good. Vooosh! And the rest of the street is the same as the shop. The whole world is nothing but a wasteland. Black sky, black earth, black nothing. Some areas are still smouldering, cooled only by the gentle snowfall. The only thing left standing is this house. Like a dark tower in the middle of a wasteland.

Pause.

Nothing left.

Pause.

No heaven visible.

Haley is asleep now. Presley gets up and goes to the window.

Presley Nothing except him. Sitting in the gutter.

Peers closer.

Oh, Haley, he looks so beautiful. Really he does. You wouldn't believe it. Come and look, Haley . . . Haley?

Presley looks to make sure Haley's asleep.
He looks back out of window.
Pause.

Presley takes step towards door.
He hesitates.
Pause.

Presely goes back to window.
He looks distraught.
Slight pause.

Presley goes back to door.
He is breathing very heavily.
Slight pause.

Suddenly, Presley unbolts door.
Slight pause.

Presley exits.
Pause.

Presley enters with Cosmo Disney. Cosmo is eighteen, pale, with blond hair, and a menacing, angelic beauty. He is wearing a long black leather overcoat buttoned up to the neck, black trousers, and black patent-leather shoes.

Presley is trying to help Cosmo inside but – as Cosmo shies away from Presley's touch – the effect is more of shooing him into the room.

Cosmo is hunched over, obviously still in pain.
He stands in middle of room.

35

Presley rebolts the door.
Cosmo vomits.
Presley stares.

Slight pause.

Cosmo That's your fault, that is. Forcing me in here. Knew I was going to puke. Always do.

Presley . . . Why?

Cosmo Have to get it out of my system.

Stares at Presley suspiciously.

You ill?

Presley No.

Cosmo You look it.

Presley Well, I'm not.

Cosmo I'm ain't a lover of illness, me. Sick things. Germs getting into my bloodstream. I've never had anything wrong with me. Want it to stay that way.

Indicating vomit.

You should clear that up, old son.

Presley goes to kitchen and fills a bucket with water.
Cosmo looks round room, sniffs a few times.
Slight pause.

Presley returns with bucket and dishcloth and gets to his knees. He stares at the vomit.

Cosmo goes to window.

Cosmo See me from here, did you?

Presley Yeah.

36

Cosmo Why d'you come out? Feel sorry for me, did you? Think I was a boy? A boy in need?

Presley Something like that.

Cosmo Well, you was wrong. I ain't no boy.

Slight pause.

Wanted to touch me, did you?

Presley No.

Cosmo Keep it that way. Don't like being touched, me. Don't like it at all. Not by another geezer. Not even by the one I was with. See him?

Presley Yeah.

Cosmo He's gone to get our car. Parked it earlier, then forgot where it was. Could be walking the streets for hours. Not his fault. His brain ain't all it should be. He'll come back. Has to. I'm like a magnet to him. The North Pole in the compass of his life.

Stands beside Presley.

You praying or what?

Slight pause.

Won't kill you. Only vomit. Won't stain. Ain't curry.

Presley starts cleaning up the vomit.
Cosmo sniffs.
Pause.

Cosmo sniffs Presley.

Presley What . . . what's wrong?

Cosmo You stink.

Presley Of what?

37

Cosmo Chocolate.

Presley What kind?

Cosmo What d'you mean what bloody kind? Chocolate's chocolate.

Presley I eat a lot of chocolate.

Cosmo Can tell. Look at your teeth.

Presley What's wrong with them?

Cosmo They're rotten.

Presley They're not.

Cosmo When was the last time you looked in a mirror? They're all black. Like you've been eating liquorice.

Presley I hate liquorice.

Cosmo Tell your teeth that.

Presley has cleared up the vomit now.
    He takes bucket to kitchen.
    Slight pause.

Cosmo Your eyes are pretty bloodshot too.

Presley rushes out of kitchen.

Presley My eyes are pretty!

Cosmo Pretty bloodshot, I said. You get enough sleep?

Presley Plenty. I take tablets.

Cosmo Well, that explains it, old son. Tablets ain't real sleep. That's chemical sleep. Your skin's suffering, you know.

Presley My skin?

Cosmo All pale and pasty. You need some fresh air. You're an unhealthy human being, Mr Chocolate. You know what you need? A good scrub. You've been hibernating too long, that's your trouble.

Presley I'm not hibern –

Cosmo Now take me for instance. How do I look?

Presley Oh . . .

Cosmo Go on. Spit it out!

Pause.

Presley Lovely.

Cosmo Just lovely?

Presley Very lovely.

Cosmo Just very lovely? Oh, you can do better than that. Shall I tell you what I am?

Presley What?

Cosmo Perfect. Come here, Mr Chocolate.

Presley slowly approaches Cosmo.

Cosmo Look at my eyes. Are they clear? Are the whites white and the blues blue?

Presley Yeah.

Cosmo And my skin? Any pimples or scars? Any blemishes of any shape, size or description?

Presley No.

Cosmo And my hair? Is it glistening and healthy and redolent of a stallion?

Presley Yeah.

Cosmo And in my gob.

Opens mouth.

Presley gazes in Cosmo's mouth.

Presley Wonderful.

Cosmo Not one filling. Perfect white, shiny, healthy teeth. And my body. Look . . .

Presley goes to touch him.

Cosmo Don't touch! I've warned you. Don't like being touched by men. Just use your eyes. Does my body look hard and muscular and totally fat-free?

Presley Oh, yeah.

Cosmo Bet you're jealous.

Presley I am.

Cosmo How jealous?

Presley Very jealous.

Cosmo Knew you would be. People are. Look at my hands. Ain't they perfect? Perfect nails. Perfect knuckles. Smooth. White. Slender. Shall I tell you something? I ain't never broken a bone.

Presley No?

Cosmo Not one. How many you broke?

Presley I . . . can't remember.

Cosmo But you must have broken one or two. Am I right?

Presley I suppose.

Cosmo Course I am. Jesus, your breath reeks.

Presley Of chocolate?

Cosmo Nah. Just . . . reek.

Presley Shall I clean my teeth?

Cosmo Might be an idea.

*Presley goes into kitchen and starts to clean teeth.
Cosmo goes to table and looks at bars of chocolate.
Slight pause.*

*Cosmo notices bottle of medicine and picks it up.
Presley sees him from kitchen.*

Presley Don't touch that!

Cosmo Why?

Presley Just don't!

Cosmo Weren't going to steal it.

Presley It's Mummy and Daddy's medicine.

Cosmo puts bottle down.

Cosmo They ill? They ill in this house? Is it contagious?
Germs in spit?

Presley No.

Cosmo Why not?

Presley They're dead.

Cosmo When they die?

Presley Years ago.

Cosmo And you've still got their fucking medicine?

Presley That's right.

Cosmo Why?

Presley Their lips always tasted of the medicine. They would kiss us goodnight. The taste gave us pleasant dreams.

Cosmo goes to exit. As he reaches door and touches first bolt –

Haley (*loudly, in her sleep*) Mummy!

Cosmo What the fuck!

Presley (*from kitchen*) Don't be scared.

Haley Daddy!

Cosmo Who the . . .?

Presley It's my sister.

Haley Where are you?

Cosmo sees Haley for the first time.

Cosmo Where'd she come from?

Presley She's asleep.

Haley I've lost you. I've lost you.

Presley returns from kitchen.

Cosmo Nearly gave me a bloody heart attack, didn't she.

Presley I'll get you a glass of water.

Presley returns to kitchen.
  Slight pause.

Cosmo takes off his overcoat, staring at Haley. Underneath overcoat Cosmo is wearing a bright red, rhinestone and sequin jacket. It is dazzling in the colourless room. He also wears white shirt and black bow tie. He puts overcoat over back of unoccupied armchair.

Cosmo What's she sucking?

Presley (*from kitchen*) A dummy dipped in Mummy and Daddy's medicine. It soothes her.

Cosmo She ain't sick, is she?

Presley No, no. She's taken a sleeping tablet.

Cosmo But that's no good. I told you. Chemical sleep. No wonder she's having nightmares.

Presley returns with a glass of water and puts it on table. He notices Cosmo's jacket and is riveted by it.

Presley Bright jacket.

Cosmo Eh?

Presley Your jacket. Bit of a bobby-dazzler.

Cosmo Wear it for work.

Presley For *work*?

Cosmo Yeah.

Presley What d'you do, then?

Cosmo That's my business.

Presley Are you a magician?

Cosmo Nah.

Presley A singer?

Cosmo Nah.

Presley Do you make cars?

Cosmo Nah. Got a car, though.

Presley Where is it?

Cosmo I told you. The one I was with has gone to look for it. He parked it and forgot where.

Presley Because his brain ain't all it should be.

Cosmo That's right. Good boy.

Presley Am I a good boy?

Cosmo Yeah, yeah.

Presley Dad used to pat me on the head when he called me a good boy.

Presley steps up to Cosmo and lowers his head ready for a pat.

Cosmo What the fuck you up to? I told you. I don't like touching. Why don't you keep watch at the window for the car?

Presley hesitates. Then, reluctantly, goes to window.

Presley How will I know it's your car?

Cosmo is staring at Haley.

Pause.

Presley What colour is it?

Cosmo What you prattling on about?

Presley Your car. What colour?

Cosmo Beige.

Presley We used to have a beige car. Daddy used to say –

Notices Cosmo is about to touch Haley's hand.

Don't touch her!

Cosmo Only a finger.

Presley It might scare her.

Cosmo She's asleep.

Presley Might wake her, then scare her. You're not supposed to disturb a sleepwalker or talker.

Cosmo But she ain't walking or talking.

Presley That's not the point.

Slight pause.

Your water's on the table.

Cosmo goes to the table and sits down. He moves chair to see Haley better. He absently takes mouthful of water. Then spits it back into glass.

Cosmo Jesus!

Stares at water.

There's things alive in this!

Presley Always like that.

Cosmo Don't make it all right.

Presley Dad used to say tap water was the best drink in the world.

Cosmo How long's he been dead?

Presley Years.

Cosmo Yeah, well, a lot can happen in years.

Presley Not necessarily. Sometimes . . . nothing happens.

Cosmo is gazing at Haley again.
Slight pause

Presley We used to have a car.

Cosmo So you bloody said.

Presley Dad used to say there was nothing like the smell of a new car. Freshly cracked leather. Polish on dashboard.

Slight whiff of wax and petrol. Nothing to beat it.
Someone I went to school with – he bought a Porsche.
Drove it right down the street and parked it outside his
mum's door. She came out and squealed. Sat in the car.
Other neighbours came out to get their eyeful. My old
school friend . . . he was wearing white trousers. And a
white shirt. He didn't have a tie on. But he had a suntan.
Can you believe that? Middle of winter and brown as a
berry – You listening?

Cosmo Yeah.

Presley What did I say then?

Cosmo He had a suntan.

Presley That's right. Where d'you get a suntan in winter?

Cosmo Sun-bed. If he's got a Porsche, he's got a bloody
sun-bed.

Slight pause.

Presley You got a Porsche?

Cosmo Nah.

Presley What car you got?

Cosmo . . . Hillman.

Presley That's what we had! A beige Hillman!
Coincidence, eh? Eh?

Cosmo Yeah, yeah. Wow!

Presley The chrome was rusty. There was a hole in the
floor. When it rained our feet got wet. Mum gave us
wellingtons. It was a laugh. I can smell it now. Damp,
mouldy carpet. Something rotting somewhere. An old
sandwich or a dropped peanut perhaps. There'd be Mum
and Dad sitting up front. Talking about this and that.

Mum noticing all the shops. Me in the back seat with
Haley. Sunday afternoon rides. Roast beef stuck between
my teeth. Blanket over my legs. I would fiddle with the
tassels. Try to count them or tie them together. There
was a sticky patch and I'd try to pick it off.

Pause.

Cosmo Tell me. What's your sister's name?

Presley Tucking blanket round my legs. Like being in
a big pocket. Rubbing my hands over the seat. Leather
like cracked eggshells. Mole on the back of Mum's neck.
Hair in Dad's ears. The indicator lights going on and off,
on, off. Speedometer. Mum's blue cardigan. Dad would
look at me in the rear mirror. He'd wink. I'd try to wink
back. Never could. I was so happy in that car. Sometimes
I think of those days and I cry. I'd love to be in that car
again. Just for a few minutes. A few seconds even.

Pause.

Cosmo What's your sister's –?

Presley Later, at home, Mum'd make salmon and
cucumber sandwiches. Dad would brew a pot of tea.
I hated crusts. Dad'd said I had to eat them because they
were good for my teeth. We'd sit down and watch
television. Talk about the ride. Mum would say, 'I like
the Embankment.'

Pause.

Cosmo What's your sister's –?

Presley Dad'd dunk a biscuit in his tea and say, 'It's a
lovely place and that's a fact.'

Slight pause.

Cosmo What's –?

47

Presley Afterwards we'd have another cup of tea and Mum'd tell me to go to bed. I hated going to bed. Dad'd make me a sugar sandwich. Thick bread with lashings of butter dipped in gleaming sugar. Mixture of soft and crunchy. I'd drift into sleep with sweetness in my mouth.

Cosmo What's your sister's fucking name?

Presley Why you so bothered?

Cosmo Because I want to fucking know!

Presley You don't know *my* name. And it's *me* who's awake.

Cosmo Well, what's *your* fucking name then?

Presley stares.

Slight pause.

Cosmo What's wrong? Forgotten your name?

Presley Don't . . . have much cause to say it out loud. Feels . . . odd.

Cosmo Go on. Be a devil.

Presley You really want to know?

Cosmo I really want to know.

Presley Presley. Presley Stray.

Cosmo Congratulations. Now what's your sist –

Presley What's *your* name?

Cosmo Cosmo. What's your sister's –?

Presley Cosmo what?

Cosmo Cosmo Disney.

Presley Disney!

48

Cosmo What's wrong with that?

Presley Oh . . . nothing.

Cosmo Don't look like nothing.

Presley Just surprised me, that's all.

Cosmo What's your sis –?

Presley Don't meet many Disneys.

Cosmo Thousands in the phone book.

Presley Really? What a petrifying thought.

Cosmo What's your sister's –?

Presley Disneys of all shapes and sizes.

Cosmo TELL ME HER FUCKING NAME!

Presley HALEY!

Long pause.

Cosmo How old is she?

Presley My age.

Cosmo And what's that?

Presley Oh . . . about . . . er . . .

Cosmo About? Don't you know?

Presley I've lost count.

Cosmo Don't you have birthdays?

Presley Not since Mummy and Daddy went.

Cosmo How old were you when Mummy and Daddy went?

Presley Eighteen.

Cosmo And that was how many years ago?

Presley Ten.

Cosmo So you're twenty-eight.

Presley Must be.

Cosmo Jesus. You're ancient, Mr Chocolate.

Presley Stop calling me Mr Chocolate.

Cosmo Why?

Presley It ain't my name.

Cosmo It ain't?

Presley No. I told you my name.

Cosmo So you did.

Presley So use it. Go on. Call me by my name.

Pause.

Cosmo What was it again?

Presley Presley.

Cosmo Presley. That's right.

Presley Well, go on. Say something, then put my name at the end.

Cosmo Why?

Presley I want to hear you say it.

Cosmo But why?

Presley It'd make me feel good.

Cosmo You a homosexual?

Presley No.

Cosmo Because homosexuals like to be called by their first name.

Presley I'm not a homosexual. I just want you to say my name.

Pause.

Cosmo So. You are twenty-eight years old, are you, Presley?

Presley Yes. I am, Cosmo. How old are you, Cosmo?

Cosmo How old d'you think?

Presley Don't know.

Cosmo Guess.

Presley Can't.

Cosmo Try.

Presley I'll get it wrong.

Cosmo Try!

Presley Ten!

Cosmo Wrong. Eighteen.

Presley Well, you look like ten.

Cosmo No I don't. I might look young, but I don't look fucking ten.

Slight pause.

How come you and your sister are the same age?

Presley We're twins.

Cosmo You don't look alike.

Presley We're not identical. But we are similar.

Cosmo You ain't!

Presley We've got the same nose.

Cosmo Ain't!

Presley Have!

Stands next to Haley.

Look.

Cosmo It's different.

Presley Same hair then.

Cosmo Who you trying to kid?

Presley Look at our mouths. The shape of our lips.
They're the same

Cosmo They ain't.

Presley Are!

Cosmo Ain't!

Presley Everyone says they are.

Cosmo Everyone's wrong.

Presley Mummy and Daddy said we were two peas in
a pod.

Cosmo Mummy and Daddy were wrong.

Presley Mummy and Daddy were wrong!

Cosmo Yeah! Wrong!

Slight pause.

Presley But . . . our eyes! Our eyes are the same.

Cosmo Can't see her eyes. She's asleep. Wake her up and
I'll tell you if they're the same.

Presley Can't wake her up.

Cosmo Why not?

Presley Nothing can wake her up. Told you. Tablet.

Cosmo How can I see her eyes then?

Presley grabs hold of Haley and tries to open an eye.

Cosmo Don't do that.

Presley It's all right.

Cosmo You might hurt her.

Presley I'll be gentle.

Cosmo The eyes are sensitive things.

Presley You've got to see. See our eyes are the same.

Cosmo I believe you.

Presley Come here!

Cosmo I said I believe you.

Presley You can't see from there.

Cosmo You've got your finger in her bloody eye.

Presley She can't feel it.

Cosmo Her eyes are watering.

Presley Just look!

Cosmo Yeah! All right. I see.

Presley You agree? Our eyes are the same.

Cosmo Yeah, yeah.

Presley Say it!

Cosmo Your eyes are the same.

Presley Identical?

Cosmo Yes! Yes! Identical!

Presley lets go of Haley.

Presley We were in the womb together! Two little babies in Mummy's belly. I was born first. Then Haley. Seven minutes later. Mummy said we were the most beautiful babies in the world.

Cosmo All mummies say that.

Presley They do?

Cosmo Course they fucking do.

Presley Well, Daddy said it as well.

Cosmo Oh, well, then. Must be true.

Presley I've got a photograph. Of us as children. I'll show you.

Presley goes to chest of drawers and starts to rummage in drawer.

Cosmo What your parents die of? Heart attacks?

Presley No.

Cosmo Strokes?

Presley No.

Cosmo Cancer?

Presley No.

Cosmo Kidney failure?

Presley No.

Cosmo Car accident?

Presley No.

Cosmo Sexually transmitted diseases?

Presley No.

Cosmo Well, it wouldn't be old age. People don't die of old age any more, do they?

Presley I don't think so.

Cosmo So much makes us ill. We kiss and it kills us. I've seen photographs of what happens to people when they fall in love. Their skin falls off. Like they've been in a nuclear war or something. It's terrible, Mr Chocolate. You ever been in love?

Presley has found a box of photographs and takes it to the table.

Presley I loved Mummy and Daddy.

Sits at table.

Cosmo That don't count. Anyone else?

Presley My sister.

Cosmo That doesn't count either. Don't play games.

Presley I'm not playing games.

Cosmo Yes, you are.

Presley Oh, no, I'm not.

Cosmo Oh, yes, you are.

Presley Oh, no, I'm not.

Slight pause.

Cosmo Ever been in love with a woman other than family members?

Presley indicates Cosmo should sit next to him.

Presley Don't suppose so.

Cosmo What? Never?

Presley No.

Cosmo You've fucked women though, right?

Presley Not really.

Cosmo What d'you mean 'not really'? There's no grey area where fucking's concerned. Your dick's either stuck in or it's not stuck in.

Presley Don't be crude.

Cosmo You ever stuck it in?

Presley No!

Cosmo Not once?

Presley No, no. What's the big deal?

Slight pause.

Cosmo Ever snogged a woman?

Presley No.

Cosmo goes to sit, then –

Cosmo You ever stuck it in a bloke?

Presley No.

Cosmo You better tell me if you have. I bet that's why you helped me. Because I'm a perfect pretty boy without a filling in my head.

Presley I've never stuck it in a man.

Pause.

Cosmo goes to sit, then –

Cosmo Ever wanted to?

Presley What?

Cosmo Ever wanted to ride the chocolate highway?

Presley No.

Cosmo Sure?

Presley Sure.

Pause.

Cosmo All right then.

Cosmo sits and glances over at Haley.

Presley follows his look, then hands him one photograph at a time.

Cosmo I hate being touched by men. It happens everywhere these days. In pubs. Trains. Buses. Supermarkets. They come up behind you and rub their hand over your backside. Or they stand next to you, stand so close their knee touches your knee. When you buy something in a shop and the shopkeeper gives you change – if it's a man, he always makes sure he touches your hand. You noticed that? His fingers linger in your palm, feeling you, stroking you almost. Women don't do that. Women don't want to touch. Most women just slam the change down on the counter and leave it there for you to pick up. No finger contact there. But men . . . Oh, men are different. I hate being touched by men. And they all love to do it too. It's because I look younger than I am. They think they can get away with it. They think I'm just a boy. All men like schoolboys. That's why I never use a public toilet. Once, when I was standing at a urinal, this bloke stood beside me and actually leaned over to look at my cock. Can you believe that? I'd rather piss myself than let a homosexual see my cock. They should be gassed. Homosexuals. All of them. Or herded into one place. Like a big stadium. Have a bomb dropped on them. Do everyone a fucking favour. It's not that I'm narrow-minded or anything. We've all got a right to live. But we ain't got a right to stare at each other's private parts.

Presley You ain't looking at my photographs.

Cosmo I am.

Presley snatches photo from Cosmo.

Presley What was that one, then?

Cosmo What d'you mean?

Presley What's this photo of? If you were looking, you should know.

Cosmo You're playing games again.

Presley What's it of?

Cosmo All this chocolate can't be doing your old ticker any good.

Presley Don't change the subject. What's the photo of?

Cosmo You?

Presley No.

Cosmo Your mummy?

Presley No.

Cosmo Your daddy?

Presley No.

Cosmo Your sister?

Presley No.

Cosmo Who else is there?

Presley Our dog. Spookie.

Cosmo You had a dog called Spookie?

Presley What's wrong with that?

Cosmo It's bloody stupid.

Presley Don't say that. Dad named it. Spookie's a great name.

Cosmo Where's it now?

Presley Dead.

Cosmo Looks pretty healthy here.

Presley That's an old photo.

Cosmo How'd it die?

Presley Run over by a lorry.

Cosmo You see it happen?

Presley Yeah.

Cosmo Was there much blood?

Presley Lots. It ran in the gutter. People were staring. Spookie was under the front wheel. The lorry driver got out and shouted at me. He said it was my fault. Said I should have had it on a lead. He nearly hit me. I was so scared. Spookie's little black tail was wagging.

Cosmo That's just nerves.

Presley I know that. I ain't stupid.

Cosmo Nah?

Presley Nah.

  Pause.

Cosmo So what did Mummy and Daddy do when they found out you killed poor little Spookie?

Presley I didn't kill him!

Cosmo What they do?

Presley Bought me a bike. It was bright red with ribbons
on the handlebars. It had a bell and a rear-view mirror.
One night Dad came home from work and he gave me a
puncture outfit. It was a small, tin box full of wonderful
things. Can still remember them. Tiny rubber stickers
with holes in the middle. A tube of brown glue that
smelt of sawdust. A piece of sandpaper no bigger than a
postage stamp. And – oh, yeah, best of all – white chalk.
French chalk they called it. I'd rub the chalk between my
fingers and thumb. It glistened like crushed diamonds.
I loved my puncture outfit. It was my own little treasure
chest. Sparkling and beautiful. I loved it so much that,
when I eventually got a puncture, I didn't want to mend
it. I would rather not use my bike than spoil my perfect
puncture outfit.

Cosmo has been looking through the photographs.
He shows one to Presley.

Cosmo This your old man?

Presley Yeah.

Cosmo He looks big.

Presley He was. Big and strong. Everything was safe
when Dad was around. He made cars.

Cosmo What? All by himself?

Presley No. With his mates from the factory. Dad loved
his job. He said a job makes a man. Every Friday night
he would come home and put his wage packet on the
table. We'd sit round the table – me, Mum, Dad and
Haley – and we'd eat fish and chips. Dad'd say, 'Mind
the bones.' Afterwards Dad'd open his wage packet and
give Mum her housekeeping. What was left over went
into a glass jar. This was for Christmas and rainy days.
Dad saved all his wage packets. He didn't throw any
away. They're in a drawer over there. Want to see them?

Cosmo Not particularly.

Presley There's one thousand, three hundred and twenty-eight.

Cosmo You counted them?

Presley Of course.

Cosmo Why?

Presley To see how many there were.

Cosmo How long did it take?

Presley A whole night.

Cosmo Why count them at night?

Presley I sleep during the day.

Cosmo Why?

Presley Prefer being awake at night. Less people around.

Cosmo But your sister sleeps at night.

Presley Oh, she just sleeps.

Cosmo When she wake up?

Presley When she wants something.

Cosmo Have you always been . . . like this?

Presley Course not. Don't be stupid. When Mum and Dad were here we got up at eight o'clock in the morning. We'd have breakfast. Do the housework. Get the shopping. Watch television. Talk. Have cups of tea. Do all kinds of things. We'd go to bed at midnight.

Cosmo So when did you start being . . . like this?

Presley After Mum and Dad lost us.

Cosmo Lost us?

Presley No, left us.

Cosmo You said 'lost us'.

Presley Didn't.

Cosmo Did. You said, 'After Mum and Dad lost us.'

Presley I couldn't have said 'lost us'. That makes no sense. How could they lose us? They died.

Cosmo Ten years ago.

Presley That's right.

Cosmo They died in the same year?

Presley On the same day.

Cosmo The same day!

Presley That's right. One day they went out and never came back. We waited a very long time.

Slight pause.

They died instantly.

Cosmo Instantly! Must have been a car crash.

Presley It wasn't. I told you.

Cosmo A sheet of glass fell from a tall building and hit them?

Presley No. Nothing like that. It . . . it wasn't an accident.

Holding a photograph for Cosmo to see.

That's me and Haley. It's the only photograph of the two of us together.

Cosmo How old are you?

Presley You know that. We're twenty-eight.

Cosmo In the photograph, Mr Chocolate.

Presley Oh, six.

Cosmo What forest you in?

Presley It's not a forest.

Cosmo Looks like one.

Presley It's a reptile house in a zoo.

Cosmo You look bloody terrified.

*Presley takes the photograph from Cosmo and stares
at it.*
   Slight pause.

Presley I can still remember the snakes. One of them –
it was about . . . oh, ten feet long and as thick as my
arm. Its skin was all brown and flaking. As we watched,
it struggled out of its skin like it was an old sock. And
underneath . . . underneath was new skin. Bright red.
In another tank there was a brown mouse. It was being
pursued by a snake. Dad explained that the snake had
to eat live things in order to stay alive. There was a huge
crowd in front of the tank. Everyone was jostling for
room, trying to get a better look. One man pushed me.
Dad nearly hit him. One look at Dad was enough to
scare the man away. So we all stood there, watching,
waiting for the mouse to be caught. The mouse was so
scared. Every time the snake got close to the mouse
people cheered and said, 'Get him! Get him!' But the
mouse kept running away and hiding behind a rock. And
then . . . then the mouse didn't bother to hide any more.
It just turned its head away from the approaching snake.
It was like . . . by refusing to see it, the snake would
disappear. But the snake didn't disappear. It kept on
moving. Gliding over rocks and sand like something
liquid. When the mouse was caught it screamed. It

was then Haley went missing. She'd heard the mouse
screaming and it scared her. She'd run to another part
of the reptile house. When we found her she was crying.
She was so scared. Dad hit her and told her she was a
naughty girl. When we got home that night there was a
programme on television. About a group of people –
a cult I suppose you'd call them, who worshipped snakes.
The people said they were Christians and they read the
Gospels. But, instead of singing hymns, they danced to
rock 'n' roll. And, instead of holding Bibles, they held
snakes. Huge snakes like green car tyres looped round
their arms. They believed God came to them through
these snakes. That true believers would never get bitten.
One old woman started shaking like she was having a fit
or something. Her tongue poked out and her eyes rolled
back till there was nothing but white. And she started
talking. Talking in a language no one could understand.
The priest explained that she was talking the language of
God. But you can't fool me. One look at that woman's
face told me what language she was speaking. It was the
language of terror. And all those people holding snakes,
they might believe they were experiencing something
religious and wonderful, but I tell you – from where I was
sitting – all I could see was fear.

Pause.

Cosmo You like talking about the past, don't you?

Presley It's . . . comforting.

Cosmo Comforting! You think the past is comforting?

Presley Yeah.

Cosmo Well, you're wrong. I'll tell you what comfort is.

*Takes wad of money from pocket and throws it on
table.*

That!

Presley stares at it.

Slight pause.

Presley Money?

Cosmo Money, Mr Chocolate.

Presley And that's . . . comforting?

Cosmo Most comforting thing in the fucking world. You know what money is? Money is confidence. Let me tell you something. Once I had no confidence. Know why?

Presley Why?

Cosmo I had no money. I felt worthless. Felt like I didn't belong. That's how you feel, ain't it? Like you don't belong.

Presley I . . . don't know.

Cosmo Take my word for it. It's how you feel. Then one day I thought, 'Cosmo,' I thought, 'it's about time you bucked your ideas up, old son.' So I did. I made money. Lots and lots of lovely dosh!

Pause.

Presley What?

Cosmo What what?

Presley What d'you do?

Cosmo . . . It don't matter.

Presley It does. Tell me.

Cosmo Why d'you want to know? All you want is enough money for your chocolate. You ain't bothered about fuck-all else.

Presley I am! I'm . . . I'm interested in you, Cosmo.

Pause.

Cosmo You sure you ain't homosexual?

Presley Yes. How many more times?

Cosmo Yes you're sure you are or yes you're sure you ain't?

Presley Yes I'm sure . . . I ain't.

Cosmo I don't know, Mr Chocolate. Some things you say sound a little . . . suspect.

Presley Like being interested in you?

Cosmo That's right. Now let's get one thing clear. I do not want friends. Understand? I do not want them and I have not got any.

Presley What about the one outside? The one who's gone to get the car.

Cosmo He ain't my friend. He's my work associate.

Presley You looked very close.

Cosmo What you bloody inferring?

Presley Nothing. You just looked close.

Cosmo Just because we're both sitting in the gutter together don't mean we're close.

Presley What's his name?

Cosmo Pitch.

Presley Pitch?

Cosmo Pitchfork.

Presley Pitchfork!

Cosmo What's wrong with that?

Presley Oh, nothing.

Cosmo Don't look like nothing.

Presley It just surprised me.

Cosmo Surprise is good.

Presley You . . . you don't get many Pitchforks around. Or are there thousands of those in the phone book too?

Cosmo No idea. Ain't looked. He ain't my friend.

Slight pause.

Presley So . . . what?

Cosmo What what?

Presley What do you do?

Cosmo To earn money?.

Presley Yeah.

Cosmo Just objective interest?

Presley Just objective interest.

Cosmo stares at Presley.
Pause.

Cosmo clicks into action. He looks round him, then goes into the kitchen.
Presley watches uneasily.

Presley What . . . what you doing?

Cosmo Looking for something.

Presley What?

Cosmo We've all got them.

Presley What?

Cosmo You ... must ... have ... some ... somewhere...? Come on, my beauties.

Presley Will you tell me what you're doing, please?

Cosmo Ah! Here! Here's one. What a whopper!

Cosmo enters with whatever he's caught cupped in his hands. He smiles at Presley.

Presley smiles nervously back.

Cosmo – slowly – lets Presley peek at what he's holding.

Presley Take it away!

Cosmo Just tell me what it is. Say its name.

Presley ... Cockroach.

Cosmo That's right. Cockroach. Costs nothing. Am I right? Cockroaches are free. Am I right?

Presley Yeah.

Cosmo Come here.

Pause.

Slowly, Presley approaches Cosmo.
Cosmo parts his hands slightly.

Cosmo Look at it. Beautiful little thing. They can live on next to nothing. Two grains of soap powder will keep them alive for months.

Laughs.

Presley Why you laughing?

Cosmo Its legs are tickling me. I've got sensitive skin.

Stares at cockroach.

Oh, they're little survivors all right. In the event of a nuclear war, the cockroach alone will survive.

Presley That can't be true.

Cosmo It's true, Mr Chocolate. No one believes me but that doesn't make it a lie.

Slight pause.

I perform in pubs. In clubs. Anywhere people will pay me. Some nights I get through a hundred of these things.

Presley How do you mean?

Pause.

Cosmo eats cockroach.

Presley steps back, horrified.

Cosmo swallows cockroach and grins.

Cosmo Mmm . . . yum!

Slight pause.

Scared?

Presley Yeah.

Cosmo Why?

Presley Don't know.

Cosmo No one does. It scares them. But they love it. That's why they pay. I eat other things as well. Caterpillars. Maggots. Worms. Beetles. Moths. Goldfish. Slugs. Spiders. I suck live snails from shells. Bite wriggling eels in two. Gnaw heads from live mice. I've even eaten a live canary, Mr Chocolate.

Presley It's disgusting! You hear? Disgusting. And stop bloody calling me Mr Chocolate.

Pause.

Cosmo Why don't you eat one?

Presley Wh–what?

Cosmo A cockroach.

Presley No.

Cosmo Go on. Yum-yum.

Presley I . . . I can't.

Cosmo I'll find you one, Presley.

Presley You will?

Cosmo With my own hands.

Slight pasue.

And . . . it would please me, Presley.

Presley Really?

Cosmo Oh, yeah. Just let me find one. Shall I do that? Let me find one and we'll take it from there. That's all. No promises. How about it, Presley?

Pause.

Presley Well . . .

Cosmo Yessss!

Cosmo rushes to the kitchen.
  Slight pause.

Presley hovers uneasily.
  Slight pause.

Cosmo returns with a cockroach in his cupped hands.
  Presley backs away.

Cosmo Oooo – it's a whopper, Presley.

Presley Oh.

Cosmo Take a look.

Presley flinches away.

Cosmo Just one peek. That's all, Presley.

Presley Just . . . a peek?

Cosmo Just a peek.

Presley looks at cockroach.

Presley Oh . . . yeah.

Cosmo Looks tasty, eh?

Presley Mmm.

Cosmo Juicy.

Presley Yeah.

Cosmo Take another peek. Longer this time. Go on.

Presley looks at cockroach again.

Cosmo What d'you think?

Presley It's very . . . dark.

Cosmo That's right.

Presley Like a spit of tar.

Cosmo Ooo, yes. Never thought of it like that. Very good, Presley. What an imagination you've got.

Pause.

Go on, Presley.

Presley Eh?

Cosmo A nibble.

Presley I . . . can't . . .

Cosmo For me, Presley.

Presley I . . .

Cosmo I'll be upset if you don't.

Presley You will?

Cosmo Very.

Slight pause.

Presley Kill it first.

Cosmo Nah, nah. Has to be alive. That's the whole point.

Pause.

Presley stares at Cosmo's cupped hands.

Cosmo I'd feel very close to you, Presley. I'd feel as if we . . . shared something.

Presley Shared something?

Cosmo Something special.

Presley Like a . . . a communion?

Cosmo Yeah! That's it exactly. Trust you to think of the right word. It'd be a communion. Between us two. A special communion between Cosmo and Presley.

Very slowly, Presley takes cockroach from Cosmo's hands.

Cosmo Oh, Presley. You don't know how it makes me feel to see you do this.

Presley puts cockroach in his mouth and eats it.
He hates every moment.
Tries to smile.

72

Cosmo stares at him.

Pause.

Presley I need some chocolate.

Lunges for chocolate and devours a bar.

Cosmo clicks out of his 'caressing mood', grins and goes over to window.

Presley Made me feel a bit sick, Cosmo.

Cosmo Yeah. Makes me sick sometimes. What happened tonight. Suddenly got me. Razor blades in my gut. Couldn't walk. I said to Pitch, 'Pitch,' I said, 'you'll have to find the car yourself. I'm in too much agony.' Off he goes. Thought, 'In a minute I'll puke and I'll feel fine.' That's when this demented lunatic stinking of chocolate shoos me into his house. Bet you wouldn't have cleared that puke up if you knew what it was. Well, I said it wasn't curry, didn't I? Ha!

Presley You think it's funny?

Cosmo Just because I laugh don't mean it's funny.

Looks through the window.

Where the fuck is he?

Presley What does your mum think about what you do?

Cosmo Ain't got a mum.

Presley Your dad then?

Cosmo No dad either.

Presley No mum or dad?

Cosmo Nah.

Presley You must have.

Cosmo Why?

Presley How else were you born?

Cosmo I wasn't. I was hatched. Never saw my parents.
I was hatched from an egg and what you see is all I am.
Once I had the skin of a baby and now I got this skin.
I unzipped my old skin and threw it away. One day I
was shitting my nappy, the next I was earning money.
I had no childhood.

Presley I had a lovely childhood.

Cosmo It's all you've bloody had. The world is full of
people like you. Ancient children addicted to their
chocolate. Ancient children with no vocation.

Presley And what's *your* vocation?

Cosmo grabs money and –

Cosmo This!

Presley and Cosmo stare at each other.

Slight pause.

Cosmo It's a ghost train, Mr Chocolate. People love it.
Sitting there in the dark. Having the living daylights
scared out of them. Tell someone there's a photograph
of a car crash in the newspaper and what's the first thing
they do? Buy the fucking newspaper. They all say, 'Oh,
I don't want to see it.' But you know what that means?
'I *do* want to see it.' You know what we should do?
Televise public executions. A Saturday night fry-up of all
the murderers, rapists, child-molesters and homosexuals.
What a show that would be. Have the biggest audience
in the history of entertainment. And why? Because
mankind has loved to watch stuff like that since mankind
began. Public flogging, the Roman Coliseum, bear-baiting,

torture, crucifixion, Bedlam, bull-fighting, hunting, snuff-movies, the atom bomb. They're all part of the same thing. Man's need for the shivers. Afraid of blood, wanting blood. We all need our daily dose of disgust. That's all. Nothing incredible . . . You know what *is* incredible? How easy it is to stop living. Not to die, but to stop being alive. There's nothing incredible apart from that. No mystery. No magic. No dreams. No miracles. Nothing. Just freak accidents and freaks. Darwin got it all wrong, you see. Fitness has got fuck-all to do with it. It's survival of the sickest. That's all. You know why the ghost train is so popular? Because there ain't any ghosts. Once you've learnt that you can make a fucking fortune.

Presley But I don't want a fortune.

Cosmo Ain't you ever wanted anything?

Slight pause.

Presley I wanted to be an astronaut. When I was a kid –

Cosmo (*overlapping*) Oh, Jesus, what have I started? Can't you talk about anything else? I don't care about your fucking childhood.

Presley (*overlapping, continuing impervious*) – I had this book with photographs of the moon and stars. But what I liked best were the astronauts. I liked their space suits. All silver and sparkling, covered in tubes and wires and flashing lights. And the way they walked on the moon. Nothing to hold them down.

Cosmo (*overlapping*) I'm not bothered . . . I'm not interested . . . I'm not concerned . . . What a pathetic specimen you are . . . You know what your life is to me? One big yawn. That's what.

Presley (*overlapping*) And I like the names they gave
things: Saturn Five, Lunar Module, Apollo Thirteen.
Apollo Thirteen was the unlucky one. The astronauts
were trapped inside a capsule. Floating in orbit.

Cosmo (*overlapping*) I wish you were floating in fucking
orbit.

Presley (*overlapping*) Unsure if they would ever come
back to Earth. The whole world bit its nails and prayed.
Everyone said how brave the astronauts were. But it
didn't seem brave to me. Just floating off in that silver
spaceship.

Cosmo (*overlapping*) What a waste of oxygen you are.
You're sick. Know that? You are most definitely not all
there. You should be locked away.

Presley (*overlapping*) Wearing silver space suits. Just
floating away. Into dark silence. Where no one could
bother you. No, it's not so bad. I'd rather do that than
risk re-entry. Risk being burnt to a frazzle. Floating away
seems preferable to that.

Cosmo How can someone like you have such a sister?
Should be against the law.

Presley It was at that time I discovered the most
beautiful word in the language. It was in one of the
newspapers. The article said it was what the astronauts
might end up in. The word is so wonderful. Even the
way it feels in the mouth is special. Can you guess what
it is?

Slight pause.

Well?

Cosmo Well what?

Presley What is it? The most beautiful word.

Cosmo No idea.

Presley Guess.

Cosmo You and your fucking games. Just tell me.

Presley No. Guess. It's what the astronauts could have ended up in.

Slight pause.

Cosmo Space?

Presley No.

Cosmo Sea?

Presley No.

Cosmo Trouble?

Presley No.

Slight pause.

Cosmo Stratosphere?

Presley Good try.

Slight pause.

But no.

Cosmo Well, what then?

Pause.

Presley Oblivion.

Pause.

Ain't that the best? Oblivion.

Haley (*calling in sleep*) No!

Cosmo Jesus! She's off again.

Haley Find them! Keep looking! Find them!

Cosmo What did you say she keeps prattling on about?

Presley The day in the reptile house. When the sound of the screaming mouse scared her and she ran away.

Haley Mummy! Daddy!

Cosmo kneels beside Haley.

Cosmo Have you noticed how gorgeous people look when they're petrified!

Haley Hold my hand!

Cosmo goes to hold her hand.

Presley She ain't talking to you!

Cosmo You sure?

Presley Yes.

Cosmo Pity.

Pause.

The dummy's come out of her mouth.

Presley I'll put it back.

Presley tries to put dummy in Haley's mouth.
Haley spits it out.
Presley tries again.
Haley spits it out.
Presley smells dummy.

Presley She's sucked all the medicine off.

Haley They've got to be somewhere! Find them! Find them!

Presley dips dummy in medicine bottle.

Cosmo She's getting frantic.

Presley puts freshly soaked dummy into Haley's mouth.
Haley sucks it eagerly, calms down.

Presley She's been panicky all night. Even when she was awake. I had to do everything to calm her.

Cosmo The tablets?

Presley Of course.

Cosmo And chocolate?

Presley Naturally. And I had to describe what it was like outside as well.

Cosmo What? The street?

Presley That's right. Only we invent a new world. We imagine it's after the nuclear holocaust and we're the only two left alive.

Slight pause.

Cosmo What . . . what d'you say?

Presley Told you.

Goes over to window.

I describe it.

Cosmo Describe it to me.

Presley Why?

Cosmo I want to hear it.

Presley There's no point.

Cosmo Yes there is.

Presley Oh, no, there isn't.

Cosmo Oh, yes, there is.

Presley Oh, no, there isn't.

Slight pause.

Cosmo I. Want. To. Bloody. Hear. It.

Pause.

Presley Say, 'Please.'

Cosmo Please.

Presley Say, 'Please, Presley.'

Slight pause.

Cosmo Please, Presley.

Presley Say, 'Please, Presley, tell me what it's like outside.'

Pause.

Cosmo Please, Presley, tell me what it's like outside.

Long pause.

Presley Why?

Cosmo JUST FUCKING DO IT!

Presley All right! All right! Sit down, then.

Cosmo sits at table.

Pause.

Cosmo Well? What you waiting for?

Presley You have to ask me questions.

Cosmo What questions?

Presley What things look like.

Cosmo What's it look like?

Presley No, no, no. That's not right. You have to begin with the sky.

Slight pause.

Cosmo What does the sky look like?

Presley It's black. A sheet of dark cloud obscures everything. No heaven visible.

Cosmo No heaven visible!

Presley No stars. No moon. No comets. Nothing.

Pause.

Ask me if it's snowing.

Cosmo Is it snowing?

Presley Slightly.

Pause.

Now the street.

Cosmo What does the street look like?

Presley You remember the corner shop? The one where we got all our shopping. Where the shopkeeper called Mummy, 'Mrs Stray' and always asked how Daddy was? Well, it's gone. Totally and utterly. Nothing left except scorched wood and blistered glass. It's been razed to the ground.

Cosmo is listening, enthralled. As he listens he dreamily opens a bar of chocolate and starts to eat.

Presley And the shopkeeper? The one who used to say, 'Hello, Mrs Stray. How's Mr Stray?' He's gone as well. Burnt to nothing. Incinerated. One flash of light and – vooosh! He didn't exist any more. Everything is a wasteland. Black sky. Black earth. Black nothing. Some areas are still smoking, cooled only by the gentle snowfall. And we're the only two left. And this house is the only one standing. Like a . . . a dark tower in the middle of a wasteland.

Cosmo Why're we still alive, then?

Presley Because we were good children.

Pause

Cosmo What happened to your mummy and daddy, Presley?

Cosmo and Presley stare at each other.

Long pause.

Presley I have this recurring nightmare: I wake up one morning and all my teeth have fallen out. They're lying on my pillow like bits of broken china. I get up and look at my reflection in the mirror. I've aged seventy years. Suddenly I'm an old man. I go to comb my hair and it falls out by the roots. I'm so scared. I go to see Mummy and Daddy and they scream. They don't recognise me. They say, 'What have you done with our son?' And I say, 'I *am* your son. It's me. Don't you see?' But they throw me out of the house. Mummy is crying and Daddy is shouting. I'm standing on the freezing cold pavement and I'm naked. My cock is tiny and shrivelled and I'm shitting myself. It runs down my legs like brown worms. People stop and stare. An old woman comes up to me and hits me round the head with her handbag. She says, 'You should be ashamed. Exposing yourself in public like this. A man of your age. A child might see you.' And I say, 'But I *am* a child. I'm a boy. I'm not a man. Please believe me.' And she takes a bar of chocolate from her handbag. She holds it under my nose. The smell excites

me. It starts to give me an erection. I know that if I get
stiff she'll think I'm a man. So I try to stay soft. I think
to myself, 'Stay soft, stay soft, stay soft.' But the smell of
the chocolate is getting to me. I get a throbbing erection.
'You see!' says the old woman. 'You *are* a man!' I run
away. My cock scrapes across the tarmac. The helmet
gets grazed and cut. It leaves a trail of blood behind me.
As I pass the newspaper stand I see a headline. It says,
'THE PITCHFORK DISNEY STRIKES AGAIN.' I pick
up a copy of the newspaper and read. A murderer –
calling himself the Pitchfork Disney – is killing children.
He sexually abuses them, then stabs them to death with
a pitchfork. Afterwards he puts a rubber model of a
cartoon character on the mutilated body. In the
newspaper there's a full-colour photograph of a blood-
spattered cartoon mouse. The Pitchfork Disney has
vowed to kill all the children in the world. There's a
photofit picture of what the police think the murderer
looks like. He's very handsome. A perfect face. Like a
Hollywood movie star. Sun tan, sparkling teeth,
glistening eyes, shiny hair. I run down the street. I'm
very scared. Every time I hear footsteps I think it's the
Pitchfork Disney coming to get me. Suddenly I'm feeling
very cold. I've got to buy some clothes. I rush into
a clothes shop and ask for a suit. A young boy is serving.
He says, 'You can't possibly get into a suit with an
erection like that.' I tell him I know but I don't know
how to get rid of it. He says, 'Sit down and relax.'
So I sit down and the young boy takes my cock in his
hands. He starts to rub it up and down. I'm enjoying it
but I don't want to. I beg him to stop but he doesn't.
He says, 'Don't worry. This is just a Saturday job. I've
got to earn money somehow.' Then I come. It spurts over
the face of the boy. I apologise. The boy says it doesn't
matter and he gives me a suit to put on. The suit is far
too small. 'I need a bigger one,' I tell him. 'It's the

biggest we've got,' the boy says. 'This is a childs' clothes shop.' I tell him, 'I am a child.' 'Don't make me laugh,' says the boy. So I leave the shop. As I walk through the revolving doors, someone else comes in. It's a man. He has a perfect face. Like a Hollywood movie star. Sun tan, sparkling teeth, glistening eyes, shiny hair. And he's holding a pitchfork in one hand and a rubber model of a cartoon mouse in the other. It's the killer. The Pitchfork Disney. But I don't do anything. I'm too scared. I leave the shop. I stand on the pavement outside. Stare through the window. I watch the Pitchfork Disney walk up to the boy. He pushes the boy to the ground. He kneels. He sticks a finger into the boy. The boy is screaming and screaming. I want to help but I don't. I just watch. Then the Pitchfork Disney stands up. Grabs the pitchfork. And stabs the boy through the neck. The boy screams. Blood spurts over suits and pyjamas. The murderer stabs the boy in the chest. In the stomach. In the legs. In the arms. In the eyes. Again and again the gleaming pitchfork pierces the boy's body. There's so much blood. When the boy is dead the Pitchfork Disney puts the rubber mouse on the corpse and leaves. As he walks past me our eyes meet. I'm so scared. 'Kiss me,' says the Pitchfork Disney. 'No,' I say. 'Kiss me,' he says again. 'You know you want to.' And I do want to. He's so attractive. I want to kiss his lips. I hate myself for wanting to kiss him. But I do. I can't help it. He takes a step towards me. I feel his breath on my lips. He smells sweet and warm. Like chocolate. Slowly, our lips touch. I kiss him. My mouth opens. I feel his tongue nuzzle into my mouth. I hadn't expected this. I've never had a stranger's tongue in my mouth before. I jump back and vomit in the gutter. The Pitchfork Disney is insulted. He says, 'How dare you vomit when I kiss you. I'm going to kill you for that.' And he aims his pitchfork at my heart. I run. He chases me. I run into a main road without looking. I don't look left or right or anything. A lorry has to swerve to miss me. Screeching car tyres. Brakes screaming. The lorry crashes into a school. The trailer cracks open and the contents spill over the pavement. Toxic waste! The lorry is carrying toxic waste! It spurts over my body. I feel it burning into my flesh. I'm screaming and yelling. I fall to the ground. My hands splash into the toxic waste. The skin falls away like soggy, pink gloves. An ambulance arrives and takes me to hospital. I'm wheeled straight into surgery. A doctor looks at me and says, 'There's nothing left of your face. Nothing. But don't worry. We'll give you a new one.' And he gives me an injection to knock me out. Only it doesn't. I'm lying there and I can feel everything: the scalpel slicing through my skin. Digging out eyes. Cutting lips. Nipping gums. I'm so scared. I try to yell out but I can't move. All I can do is lie there and suffer the agony. They finish the operation and take me to a ward. My head is wrapped in bandages. The ward is full of children. All of them have holes in their bodies somewhere. The nurse explains that I'm in a ward full of children who have been attacked by the Pitchfork Disney but managed to get away. The doctor comes in and says, 'Now it's time to remove your bandages.' He unwinds the bandages. He holds a mirror in front of me and tells me to take a look. I stare at my reflection. A perfect face. Like a Hollywood movie star. Sun tan. Sparkling teeth. Glistening eyes. Shiny hair. They've given me the face of the Pitchfork Disney. Suddenly, all the children are pointing at me. 'It's him!' they cry. 'It's him! The Pitchfork Disney!' I jump out of bed and run out of the ward. The children are chasing me. They chase me into the street. People look and stare. The children keep screaming. 'It's the Pitchfork Disney! The Pitchfork Disney!' Everyone in the street starts to chase me. They want to kill me. The whole world hates me and there's nothing I can do about it. The whole world is chanting, 'Die! Die! Die!' They pick up broken bottles. Sticks. Anything to hit me with. Some are holding machine guns and chainsaws. They're waving these weapons in the air. They want to hack me to pieces. I'm running as fast as I can. My feet are torn to shreds. My toenails are ripped off. Police join in the chase. Tanks. Helicopters. Harrier jets. I'm so scared. I run and run and run. Heart pounding. Sound of blood in ears. Then they're on me. The whole world is on me. Stabbing me. Cutting me. Chopping me. Hacking. Peeling. Ripping. I scream, 'I'm not the Pitchfork Disney! I'm a little boy!' Someone in the crowd says, 'Skin him! Skin him alive!' And the crowd cheers. They want to watch. They're yearning to see me suffer. They start to flay me. Peeling my skin to reveal blood. Muscles. Veins. The blood makes me slippery. I slide out of their grasp and run. I run into an army air base. A gleaming silver plane is in front of me. The plane has one word written on it: 'SUGARLOVE'. I jump onto the wing of the plane. Then into the cockpit. The crowd is on the runway now. I pull a lever. Propellers spin round. The plane begins to move. I fly up to the clouds. I've never been in a plane before. Any minute I might crash and I haven't got a parachute. I'm so scared. I look behind me. Hundreds of planes are after me. Like a swarm of locusts. A black button in front of me. On it is written the single word: 'MEDICINE'. I know that if I press the button I will drop a nuclear bomb. But I have no choice. I have to do something. I press the button. The bomb falls from the belly of the plane. It lands below me. A gigantic, luminous mushroom cloud rises to engulf the plane. I lose control of the plane. It crashes. The plane is destroyed. But I'm not hurt. I climb from the wreckage. Other bombs are dropping now. I hear explosions and see flashes of white light and mushroom clouds everywhere. I know I've stared a nuclear war and humanity will be destroyed. But I had to save my own life. Everything is devastated around me. Clouds start to cover the sky. The explosions stop. Things get very still. I know I am the last living thing in the world. My toes the last toes. My shins the last shins. My knees the last knees. My belly the last belly. My heart the last heart pumping the last blood round the last veins and arteries. My fingers are the last fingers. My hands the last hands. Last neck. Last lips. Last nose. Eyes, eyelashes, eyelids, eyebrows, the last of their kind. Teeth, last. Tongue, last. Ears, last. Everything that is me is the last of everything. I am unique. The last to see. The last to touch. The last to smell. When I have stopped seeing and touching and smelling then all of these things will cease to be. And my voice. My voice is the last voice. I am the sole survivor. So I sit in the darkening wasteland and these things give me comfort. Who needs other legs and arms and hearts when they can be taken from you? Who needs eyes to see when they refuse to see you? Who needs other fingers when they refuse to touch you? Who needs other voices to speak when they refuse to say the right things? And then . . . then it starts to snow. The snow lands on my skinless body. It gives me a new skin. My wounds are healed. The nuclear snowfall transforms me. I rise from the ashes and I am perfect. I am a boy again.

Gradually, the window behind Presley lights up with approaching car headlights. The light is pure white and blindingly dazzling.
   A car parks outside.
   Pause.

The car sounds its horn.

Long pause.

Cosmo He's come back for me.

Presley Yeah.

Pause.

Car beeps again.

Pause.

Cosmo moves to the door.

Presley Don't.

Cosmo Don't what?

Presley Don't go.

Cosmo starts unbolting door.

Cosmo But he's waiting. Jesus! So many locks. If I leave him he's liable to get a bit panicky. He's got a nervous disposition.

Presley Please don't go.

Cosmo And I've got to get home. Curl up in bed.

Presley Don't go.

Cosmo Get my beauty sleep.

Presley Don't.

Cosmo You know, I never dream.

Finishes unbolting the door.

Uncaged!

Presley grabs Cosmo.

Presley Stay!

Cosmo Don't fucking touch me! How many more times?

Pause.

I'll tell you what. Why don't I bring Pitch in here to meet you. Say hello. Have a little party.

Presley I've let enough people in.

Cosmo There it is, you see. Once you start, where do you stop?

Cosmo waits for answer.
Presley just stares.
Pause.

Cosmo Toodle-oo then.

Presley No!

Cosmo No what?

Presley No . . . don't!

Cosmo No don't. What's that supposed to mean? You're confused, Mr Chocolate. Either I go. Or I stay with Pitch. What's it to be?

Pause.

Well?

Presley Stay.

Cosmo Somehow I knew you'd say that.

Cosmo exits.

Pause.

Car headlights go off.

Presley The sky is black. A sheet of dark cloud obscures . . . everything. No . . . no comets. Nothing. And the corner shop is . . . The whole world is . . . Black sky, black earth, black nothing . . . No heaven visible.

Cosmo and Pitchfork appear at door.
The sight of Pitchfork stops Presley in his tracks.

Pitchfork is dressed the same as Cosmo; bright red sequin jacket, etc.

89

*He has a black leather bondage mask on with holes
for eyes and mouth.
He is very tall. He has a shuffling, awkward walk.*

Cosmo and Pitchfork enter.

Cosmo Pitchfork Cavalier, meet Mr Chocolate.

Pitchfork holds out his hand for Presley to shake.

Cosmo Shake his hand, then.

Pause.

Presley stares nervously at Pitchfork.

Cosmo He wants you to shake his hand.

Presley Don't . . . don't have many visitors. Forget what
to do.

Cosmo You shake hands.

Presley Didn't shake your hand.

Cosmo Well, I don't like touching. Told you that. But
Pitch here . . . oh, he relishes physical contact. Intimacy
is second nature to him. Go on. Shake his hand. Don't
want to offend him, do you?

*Tentatively, Presley takes hold of Pitchfork's hand.
He shakes it quickly, then steps back.*

Cosmo Call that a handshake?

Presley What d'you mean?

Cosmo That weren't a handshake, Mr Chocolate. That
was a hand touch. Now, shake hands with him properly
before you upset him.

Pitchfork's hand is still outstretched.

Presley But I –

Cosmo Do it! Three times up and three times down! That's what I call a real handshake. Do it! Do it!

Slowly, reluctantly, Presley steps forward and holds Pitchfork's hand again.
Presley lifts it up and down three times.
Cosmo counts each one.

Cosmo One . . .! Two . . .! Three . . .!

Presley takes a step back from Pitchfork.
Pitchfork puts his hand down.

Presley His hands are very soft.

Cosmo Baby-soft you might say?

Presley Yeah.

Cosmo Soft as a baby's bottom even?

Presley Yeah.

Cosmo And that's just what he is! A big, contented baby.

Pitchfork holds out both his hands.

Presley I've already shaken his hands.

Cosmo He knows that, Mr Chocolate. He wants you to *look* at his hands now. To show you how soft they really are.

Presley But I've looked.

Cosmo Look again!

Presley steps forwards and looks at Pitchfork's hands.

Presley Yeah. They do look soft. Does he use cream?

Cosmo Never! What an idea, Mr Chocolate. You absolutely sure you ain't a homosexual?

Presley No.

Cosmo No you ain't or no you ain't sure?

Presley No I . . . ain't.

Cosmo Well, you do make me wonder sometimes. Hand cream indeed! We're working boys. What would he want hand cream for?

Slight pause.

Presley So what does he do?

Cosmo He works with me. I told you. We're associates.

Presley Does he eat . . . things as well?

Cosmo No. He don't have to. Not with a face like his.

Presley What's wrong with his face?

Cosmo Oh, it's . . . what can I say . . .? How can I describe it? . . . Imagine your nightmare, Mr Chocolate.

Presley . . . Yeah.

Cosmo Now multiply it by the number of stars in the universe. That's how bad his face is.

Presley So . . . what does he do in the act?

Cosmo I take it off.

Presley What?

Cosmo His mask.

Presley That's all?

Cosmo That's enough, believe me. I've seen women faint and grown men vomit. Earns a fortune. He walks onto the stage, sings a little ditty, then I go to take his mask off.

At an invisible audience.

92

I look round at the audience and I say, 'What shall I do . . .? Shall I take it off . . .? Have you all sunk that low?' And they tell me what to . . .

Looks at Presley.

I'll tell you what! Why don't we give you a little show!

Presley A what?

Cosmo A show! Let's see how human you really are!

Presley No . . .

Cosmo What?

Presley No.

Pause.

Cosmo You know what that 'no' means, don't you, Mr Chocolate?

Presley What?

Cosmo Yes!

Putting chair in middle of room.

Pitch! Up!

Slowly, Pitchfork walks to the chair. He lifts his leg and tries to get up. He obviously finds it difficult, and continues to stumble as Cosmo begins his speech to an invisible audience –

Cosmo Ladies and gentlemen! Thank you for coming to our little show.

Presley is concerned for Pitchfork.

Presley He can't do it.

Cosmo All we want to do is entertain you.

Presley Help him.

Cosmo Make you laugh, make you shiver.

Presley He's going to hurt himself!

Cosmo What else is there? Welcome to the ghost train!

Presley (*louder*) He's going to hurt himself.

Cosmo (*angrily*) He can fucking do it!

Presley He can't! Look at him!

Pitchfork is still struggling to get up on the chair.

Cosmo I've already told you your trouble, Mr Chocolate. And this proves it! You have got to stop caring too much!

Presley But look at –

Cosmo No 'buts', Mr Chocolate. If I can say he can get up on the chair, he can get up on the chair.

Pitchfork knocks chair over.

Cosmo Pitch! Get up!

Pitchfork struggles frantically.

Presley . . . Don't . . . oh, don't . . .

Cosmo Get up! Get up! Get up!

Presley Don't.

Cosmo Be quiet! Up! Up! Up! Up! Up! Up! Up!

Finally, Pitchfork manages to get up on chair.

Cosmo There! You see!

At invisible audience.

And now – ladies and gentlemen – to begin our little show, my associate here will sing a charming little lullaby entitled, 'Cradle Me to Heaven'. Over to you, Pitch.

Cosmo steps back and watches Pitchfork . . .

For a moment, Pitchfork stands on the chair, his hands twitching. His mouth opens . . . At first, no sound comes out. Pitchfork begins to shake. His mouth opens wider. He wobbles on the chair. His hands shake more violently . . . Then . . .
A noise comes from between his lips: a terrible howl – half-human, half-animal. It has a strange, hypnotic, barbaric beauty . . .

Cosmo grins.

Pitchfork continues his 'song'. The only words that can be vaguely discerned are 'cradle' and 'heaven'.

When the song is over Pitchfork closes his mouth and stops twitching.
Pause.

Cosmo Wasn't that moving, ladies and gentlemen!

Starts clapping.

Let's hear it for Pitch!

Presley is not clapping. He is still staring at Pitchfork, shocked by the song. Cosmo notices Presley not clapping.
Cosmo walks up to Presley and starts clapping in front of his face.

Cosmo Go on! Clap! Clap! Clap! Clap! Clap!

Gradually, Presley begins to clap.
Presley and Cosmo stand applauding Pitchfork for a while.
Pitchfork bows.

Cosmo Beneath this mask, ladies and gentlemen, is . . . oh, how can I describe it? It is your worst nightmare.

Pitchfork is sitting on chair now.

Presley What . . . what're you going to do?

Cosmo Take off the mask.

Presley No.

Cosmo That means, 'yes'.

Presley No. It means no.

Cosmo glances at Presley.
  Pause.

Cosmo It's not wrong to admit it, Presley. Honest. Trust me. It's only human. Admit you're human, Presley. Tell me you want to see it?

Presley I . . . I . . .

Cosmo Tell me . . .

Presley I . . .

Cosmo Say it.

  Pause.

Presley Yes! Let me see!

Cosmo There. Told you. You're the same as all the rest.

Presley You *made* me say it.

Cosmo You want to be part of the ghost train after all. Saying you want to see his face is the price of entry.

Pitchfork has noticed Haley. He shuffles towards her, his hands outstretched, intent on touching her.

Cosmo Only you're worse than the others, Mr Chocolate. You say 'yes', then deny it. You don't deserve to see his face.

Haley makes a noise as Pitchfork touches her.

Presley Tell him to stay away!

Pitchfork takes Haley's hand.

Cosmo You tell him.

Presley He mustn't touch her.

Cosmo Tell him then.

Presley Don't touch her.

Cosmo Oh, you'll have to do better than that. Told you. He's a little deaf.

Pitchfork brings Haley's hand to his lips.

Presley Don't touch her.

Cosmo Louder, Mr Chocolate.

Presley Don't.

Cosmo Louder.

Presley Can't you tell him? He's your friend.

Cosmo He's not my friend! How many more times?

Presley But he listens to you.

Cosmo That's because I speak loud enough.

Presley I don't want you to . . . Don't . . . touch . . .

Suddenly, Pitchfork pulls Haley from the chair and up into his arms.
He holds her tight against his chest.
Haley lets out a cry in her sleep.

Presley I don't like this.

Cosmo So attract his attention. Say his name. Pitch.

Presley Pitch.

Cosmo Not at me, Mr Chocolate. At *him*.

Presley Pitch.

Cosmo Louder.

Presley Pitch! Pitch!

Cosmo Should warn you, though.

Presley What?

Cosmo He's got a shocking temper. I saw him gnaw someone's ear off once. Quite remarkable. Especially when you consider he hasn't got a tooth in his head.

Presley Oh, what's he doing?

Cosmo Having a boogie.

Presley Oh, no, no . . .

Cosmo I'd leave him if I were you. He'll just do a few steps, then put her down. It's how he likes his women. Unconscious.

Presley Cosmo, please –

Cosmo Want to sit in the car?

Presley Wh–what?

Cosmo Sit in the car. It's beige. And it's a Hillman. It'll be just like sitting in Mummy and Daddy's car.

Presley (*watching Pitchfork*) I don't know . . . I . . .

Cosmo Go on. You know you want to.

Presley Not now.

Cosmo Why not?

Presley I don't want to leave him with Haley.

Cosmo He won't do anything. Vital parts of him are missing. Know what I mean? He's touching her out of a sense of nostalgia. That's all.

Pitchfork stops dancing with Haley. He puts her back in her seat.

Presley rushes to Haley.

Cosmo indicates to Pitchfork that Pitchfork should eat chocolate on table.

Presley Her heart's beating very fast.

Cosmo Hearts like doing that.

Presley And she's sweating.

Cosmo I won't tell you again. You care too much.

Pitchfork sits at table and unwraps a bar of chocolate.

Presley I hope he ain't made her ill.

Cosmo From a boogie? Don't be stupid.

Presley She's susceptible to fevers.

Notices the chocolate Pitchfork is about to eat.

Oh, what's he doing now?

Cosmo All that singing and dancing must have made him peckish.

Presley Oh, stop him. Please.

Cosmo You stop him.

Presley What about his temper?

Cosmo What about it?

Presley What will he do?

Cosmo Who knows? It's a risk you take.

Presley hovers, debating whether to stop Pitchfork eating chocolate.

Presley I . . . I can't.

Pitchfork continues to eat chocolate.

Cosmo I'll tell you what, Mr Chocolate. Why don't you let Pitch drive you to the shop to get some more chocolate. Drive you in the beige Hillman.

Presley But I can't leave –

Cosmo You'll do that, won't you, Pitch? Drive Mr Chocolate to the shop?

Pitchfork nods, eating chocolate.

Presley But . . . but what about Haley?

Cosmo It's because of Haley you're doing it, Presley. To get Pitch away from her for a while. By the time you both come back – why, he'll be as calm as an electrified pig before slaughter.

Presley He will?

Cosmo And we can all sit down and nibble chockie together. You'd like that, wouldn't you?

Presley But . . . Haley . . .

Cosmo thrusts money into Presley's hands.

Cosmo Here! Take this! Buy all the chockie you need.

Presley Spend it all?

Cosmo Every penny.

Presley But it's too much.

Cosmo My treat! What's life for if we don't have our little treats. Now, you go on, Presley.

Presley But, Cosmo . . .

Cosmo What, Presley?

Presley Haley.

Cosmo I'll protect her, Presley.

Presley You will?

Cosmo With my life, Presley.

Slight pause.

Get your coat, Presley.

Presley takes overcoat from hook and puts it on.

Cosmo My! What a smart coat.

Presley You think so?

Cosmo I do, Presley. A real bobby-dazzler and that's a fact.

Presley Mum and Dad bought it for me.

Cosmo Mummy and Daddy had style, Presley. Mummy and Daddy had taste. Mummy and Daddy bought you a good coat to go to the shops to buy chockie in – Pitch!

Pitchfork stands and goes to door.

Presley I'm still not –

Cosmo Let me do this for you, Presley. It would make me feel . . . close to you.

Presley How close?

Cosmo Very close.

Presley Perhaps . . . friends almost?

Cosmo Perhaps friends almost.

Presley Because friends – they buy each other presents, don't they?

Cosmo Indeed they do, Presley.

Presley And this is your present to me.

Cosmo That's right. And it makes me feel so good to give it to you. To see your little boy's face light up. But you know the most important things friends do for each other, Presley?

Presley What, Cosmo?

Cosmo They trust each other.

Presley They do?

Cosmo They do. And if you leave me here . . . it'll prove you trust me. And I'll know that we're friends. I'll know it in my heart. So why don't you just go to the shops like a good boy?

Presley A good boy?

Cosmo A good boy.

Presley bows his head for Cosmo to pat.

Pause.

Slowly, Cosmo pats Presley's head.

Slight pause.

Cosmo indicates Pitchfork should leave.

Pitchfork exits.

Cosmo indicates Presley should follow Pitchfork.

Slight pause.

Presley follows.

Pause.

The car drives off.

Pause.

Cosmo approaches Haley.

Haley Keep looking! Keep looking! Look everywhere. Find my mummy and daddy.

Cosmo goes to touch her. Stops. Walks away. Watches her from across the room.

Haley continues to mumble, 'Mummy' and 'Daddy'.
    Pause.

Cosmo approaches again.
    Stops.
    Pause.

Cosmo paces the room.

Cosmo notices the bottle of medicine on table. He picks it up. Looks at bottle, then at Haley, then back again. Unscrews lid from bottle. Smells it. Dips finger in medicine bottle. Puts bottle on table.

Haley They must be somewhere. They can't just get lost. Something must have happened to them! Keep looking! Keep looking!

Cosmo pulls dummy from Haley's mouth. She reaches after it. He touches his medicine-coated finger to her lips. Haley begins to suck his finger. Cosmo gasps. Slowly, Haley's lips work their way up to his knuckle. Cosmo's breathing gets rapid.

Haley continues to suck. Cosmo's knees begin to give way. He is panting. His body is weakened. He gasps out loud, ecstatically. He falls to his knees. Haley sucks and sucks. Cosmo thrusts his finger into her mouth with increasing savagery. She continues sucking with increasing ferocity. Cosmo is reaching a climax. He yells out as he reaches orgasm.

Presley appears in doorway. He watches Cosmo for a while.

Pause.

Presley steps into room.

Cosmo notices Presley.

Presley I didn't go to the shop.

Cosmo . . . No?

Presley The car only drove a few yards. And then I thought –

Cosmo Where's Pitch?

Presley In the car.

Cosmo Best join him then.

Presley blocks doorway.

Presley You're a liar.

Cosmo Out the way.

Presley You said you were my friend.

Cosmo Out the fucking way!

Presley Told me to fucking trust you.

Cosmo You can't fucking trust anything, Mr Chocolate. Ain't you learnt that yet? Everyone lies and cheats to get what they want? You know what life is? Floating in a sewer in a boat made of glass. You have to learn to love the shit otherwise the journey ain't none too pleasant. In other words, this is what life thinks of you.

Sticks his finger up.
  Presley grabs finger.

Cosmo Let me go . . . Don't touch . . . Ahh . . . Don't . . .

Falls to his knees.

Presley Oh, you're scared now, eh?

Cosmo No!

Presley Tell me you're scared.

Twists Cosmo's finger.

Cosmo Ahh!

Presley Tell me you're scared.

Cosmo Ahhh . . . no.

Presley Say, 'I'm scared.'

Cosmo Ahh . . . no.

Presley Say it . . .! Say it . . .! Say it . . .!

Pause.

Cosmo I'm scared.

Presley breaks Cosmo's finger. A sickening crack.
  Cosmo screams and stares at his hand.

Pause.

Cosmo . . . What have . . .? What have you done?

Presley Get out! Get out! Get out!

Cosmo rushes out.

Pause.

Presley closes the door and is about to bolt the locks when –

Haley What's happened to you, Mummy? What's happened to you, Daddy?

Presley Oh, Haley . . .

Rushes to Haley.

Haley You were so good, Mummy. You were so good, Daddy.

Presley You were right, Haley. We must never let anyone in. Never. Where's your dummy?

Searches for dummy.

Shush, now. No, never let anyone in. Just us.

Finds dummy.

I'll dip it in some more medicine for you.

Goes to medicine.

That's all we need, Haley. Just us.

As Presley coats the dummy with medicine, the front door slowly swings open.

Pitchfork stands in doorway.

Pause.

Presley turns and sees Pitchfork.

They stare at each other.

Pause.

Presley What . . . what do you want?

Pitchfork approaches Presley.

Presley backs away, still holding medicine and dummy.

Presley Oh, no. Not me too.

Pitchfork continues to approach Presley.

Presley Don't . . . don't hurt me . . .

Backs into armchair and falls into it.

Pitchfork approaches.

Presley is whimpering with fear.

Pitchfork stands in front of Presley.

Pause.

Presley Murder.

Suddenly, Pitchfork lunges forward.

Presley flinches. Pitchfork grabs Cosmo's overcoat from the back of the armchair.

Pause.

Pitchfork walks towards door. At door, Pitchfork turns to face Presley.
Pause.

Pitchfork (*violently, very loud*) BOO!

Presley jumps, drops medicine and dummy, covers mouth with hands.

Pitchfork exits.

Presley suppresses a scream. Finally, it squeezes its way out. It is heartbreaking, terrible.

The scream wakes Haley.

Haley No! It can't be – oh, Presley! Who could've done it to them?

Presley rushes to Haley.

Presley It's all right, Haley.

Haley Mum and Dad – oh, they were so good. Who would want to hurt them like that?

Presley and Haley embrace each other.

Presley Calm down, Haley.

Haley But it makes no sense, Presley.

Presley I know, I know.

Haley There's no meaning.

Presley I know.

Haley I'm scared.

Presley Me too.

Haley I'm scared.

Presley I'm scared.

Fade to blackout.

THE FASTEST CLOCK IN THE UNIVERSE

For Dominic Vianney Murphy –
who wears the moon on his skin

Your ideas are shocking and your hearts are faint. Your acts of pity and cruelty are absurd, committed casually, as if they were irresistible. Finally, you fear blood more and more. Blood and time.

Paul Valéry

There is nothing to be said for you. Guard your secret. Conceal it under your hard plumage, necromancer.

Marianne Moore

I have felt the wind of the wing of madness.

Baudelaire

Characters

Cougar Glass
Captain Tock
Foxtrot Darling
Sherbet Gravel
Cheetah Bee

The Fastest Clock in the Universe was premièred at the Hampstead Theatre, London on 14 May 1992, with the following cast:

Cougar Glass Con O'Neill
Captain Tock Jonathan Coy
Foxtrot Darling Jude Law
Sherbet Gravel Emma Amos
Cheetah Bee Elizabeth Bradley

Directed by Matthew Lloyd
Designer Moggie Douglas
Lighting Michael Calf
Sound John A. Leonard
Artistic Director for Hampstead Theatre Jenny Topper

Act One

*A dilapidated room above an abandoned factory in the
East End of London. Many large cracks in walls. Table,
hardbacked chairs, sofa, cupboard, sideboard, window
aglow with setting sunlight, fridge, sink, gas cooker,
mirror. The main feature, however, is birds: stuffed birds,
china birds, paintings of birds, etc., giving the room an
atmosphere somewhere between museum and aviary.
Two doors: the first leading to bedroom, the second to a
corridor outside (when this second door is open another
door is visible at the end of corridor, plus a wooden
staircase that leads down, presumably to the street).*

*Cougar Glass is sitting at table. He is a young-looking
thirty-year-old, suntanned, well-built, hair jet black and
roughly styled in a quiff. He is wearing white underwear
(skimpy, stylish and very sexy) and dark glasses. In one
hand he holds a cigarette, in the other a bottle of beer.
In front of him, on the table, is a lit sun-ray lamp. It is
aimed directly at him.*

Cougar sips beer, then puffs cigarette.

Pause.

Footsteps approach down corridor. The door opens.

*Captain Tock enters. He is forty-two years old, pale,
slightly built and very balding. He is wearing a button-up
white shirt (without tie) and a (somewhat shabby) black
suit. He is holding a gold-coloured cake box.*

Captain closes door.

Pause.

Captain I've just had a shocking experience.

Cougar doesn't react.

Pause.

Captain Remember that bird I've been telling you about? The one under the bridge down the road? Caught in some wire or something?

Pause.

Captain All week it's been flapping its wings. And – Good Lord! – the squalling! Quite deafening. You know how everything echoes under that bridge.

Pause.

It was a magpie.

Pause.

Are you listening, Cougar?

Cougar flicks ash on the floor.

Captain Oh, what a petty thing to do.

Puts cake box down and gets dustpan and brush.

What do you think I am? Your skivvy?

Gets to his knees and sweeps up ash.

I've got better things to do with my time.

Cougar flicks ash on Captain's head.

Captain Oh, good Lord! Really, Cougar! Really! This kind of behaviour is just uncalled for.

Brushes himself and stands.

I've got to get things ready for your party. So don't try my patience.

Puts dustpan and brush away.

That sun-ray lamp must be eating half your brain away.
The half with consideration. I'll get you an ashtray.

Captain puts ashtray on table.

Cougar stabs out cigarette.

Captain I suppose you want another cigarette now?

Cougar grins.

Captain puts cigarette in Cougar's mouth and lights it.

Captain I adore it when you breathe deeply. I imagine
your stomach muscles tensing. Like rows of packed
walnuts.

*Cougar finishes his beer, then slams empty bottle on
table.*

Captain flinches.

Pause.

Captain Another drink now, is it?

Cougar grins.

*Captain gets bottle of beer from fridge, opens it, then
hands it to Cougar.*

Captain disposes of empty bottle.

Captain I'm not drinking any alcohol tonight, Cougar.
Party or no party. And I'm not eating any of that
birthday cake either. It's no good me taking all my
vitamins, then filling my stomach with rubbish. It wears
away my defences. And what would you do if anything
happened to me? You wouldn't find anyone else to wait
on you hand and foot. Do you want anything else?

Cougar shakes head.

Captain approaches Cougar.

Captain You sure?

Cougar nods.

Captain touches Cougar's hair.

Cougar slaps Captain's hand.

Captain retreats a few steps.

Captain Ah, now I've got your attention, I'll tell you about the magpie. Under the bridge down the road. The bird I've been telling you about. Remember? Well, children have been throwing things at it, of course. 'Leave the bird alone,' I've been telling them. 'Let it die in peace.' Would they listen? Of course not. And every day the bird got thinner and thinner. And the squalls got fainter and fainter. It must have been so beautiful once. And now it was just target practice for brutal children. When it finally died, I heaved a sigh of relief. It won't suffer any more, I thought. But it started to rot. The legs caught in the wire started to wither away.

Cougar winces.

Captain Don't worry. I'll spare you the gruesome details. I knew that – one day – the bird was going to fall. So every morning and every evening, as I walked under the bridge, I kept one eye on where I was going and one eye on that bird. Watching for the tell-tale signs of legs disintegrating. But this evening . . . this evening I didn't watch. And you know why? Because I had your birthday cake in my hands, so I had both my eyes on the pavement, in case I slipped in some moist bird droppings. And, naturally, tonight the bird fell. It missed me, I'm glad to say. But only by a few inches. Of course, in a way, I count myself lucky. It could have landed on my head. What would that have looked like? Me walking home with rotten magpie on my head.

Captain touches Cougar's hair.

Cougar slaps Captain's hand.

Captain retreats a few steps.

Captain There's an old nursery rhyme about magpies, isn't there, Cougar? Remember? A nursery rhyme or song or something. How does it go now? One . . . one for . . . sorrow. Yes. That was it. Two for joy. Three for a . . . oh, what is it? Three for a . . . girl. Yes. A girl. And four for a . . . What was four for, Cougar? Do you remember? What was four for?

Pause.

What was four for, Cougar? Four for a –

Cougar Boy.

Captain Hallelujah! I knew you were listening. A boy! Of course. A boy. Then five for silver, six for gold and seven . . . Seven, Cougar? What was seven for? Seven for a . . .?

Cougar Secret.

Captain That's right! Seven for a secret never to be told. Thank you, Cougar. That was a great help. Then eight was a wish, and nine was a kiss.

Captain touches Cougar's hair.

Cougar slaps Captain's hand.

Captain retreats a few steps.

Captain All right, all right! I can tell when you're getting irritated. That little pucker appears on your brow.

Cougar Wrinkle?

Captain No, Cougar. Not a wrinkle. A pucker. There's a difference.

Cougar Mirror!

Captain Good Lord! Shall I get the dictionary? You see a pucker is –

Cougar Mirror!

Captain gets hand mirror.

Captain If you don't want wrinkles, you should stay away from that lamp. You know what sunlight does for you. It dries you out. Turns you into a wrinkled old prune before your time.

Captain gives Cougar a mirror.

Cougar takes sunglasses off and studies his reflection.

Captain I wish I could look into the mirror with your confidence. Inspect my face with such interest and find only delight. Mirrors have never been kind to me. I even approach shop windows with caution in case my reflection springs into view. You see, I have this image in my mind of what I look like. But for some reason, it doesn't correspond with what mirrors tell me. It must be glorious to know your appearance is a source of wonder. No matter where you go people are content merely to gaze at you. That has always eluded me. I can't even say I was beautiful once.

Cougar You had hair once.

Captain Was I beautiful when I had hair?

Cougar No.

Captain Your honesty is crippling. And, by the way, you've missed a few.

Cougar Missed a few?

Captain Grey hairs. Round the back.

Cougar strains to see with mirror.

Cougar I can't see.

Captain Well, they're there.

Cougar I left the dye on for two hours. Even did my eyebrows.

Captain The eyebrows are fine. It's just the grey hairs round the back that give the game away.

Cougar Get the tweezers, Captain.

Captain I'm busy getting the party ready. What time is your guest arriving?

Cougar Same as usual.

Captain If you hadn't smashed all the clocks –

Cougar They deserved to be smashed! Fucking clocks! Nothing to do but sit there ticking!

Captain You had no right to smash them. They were mine. From my antique shop.

Cougar Junk shop!

Captain Antique shop!

Cougar You sell people's old crap!

Captain Antiques!

Cougar Junk clocks from a junk shop!

Captain Well, at least we could tell the time!

Pause.

Cougar You going to get the tweezers or what? I can't have a nineteenth birthday party with my hair turning grey.

Pause.

125

Captain goes to cupboard, gets tweezers, approaches Cougar.

Captain Turn that lamp off, then. You know how delicate my skin is.

Cougar You turn it off. I'm cooking nicely.

Captain turns lamp off, then stands by Cougar, searching for grey hairs.

Captain Your selfishness is awesome. You don't put yourself out for anyone. You're nothing but a fiend who expects everything –

Cougar Fiend! Where do you dig all these words up from?

Pause.

Captain It's too dark now.

Cougar Christ Almighty!

Captain Don't be so irritable all the time.

Captain goes to main light switch. He flicks it on. The lights flicker on and off violently.

Captain Come on, lights!

The lights continue to flicker.

Cougar One day this whole fucking building will just . . . crumble away.

The lights stay on.

Captain There!

Captain begins searching Cougar's hair again.

Cougar Hang on! Show me your fingernails.

Captain What?

Cougar Fingernails!

Captain They're fine, Cougar.

Cougar Then show me!

Captain shows Cougar his fingernails.

Cougar Oh, they're revolting, Captain. Christ Almighty! You've been biting them again. I don't know how you can just gnaw and gnaw at them like that. Look! All the skin is chewed away. They might leak at any minute. Put the gloves on.

Captain But it's hard to get a grip on the tweezers with the –

Cougar I'm not having you leak all over me, Captain. Gloves!

Captain goes to a drawer. He removes pink, rubber washing-up gloves and puts them on.

Cougar You know what you should do? Go outside and stick your fingers in some of that bird shit. That'd stop you biting your nails.

Captain resumes searching for Cougar's grey hairs.

Captain Don't be disgusting.

Cougar I'm not being disgusting. It's a good idea. There's so much shit everywhere, you might as well put it to use . . . Ouch! That hurt!

Captain Don't fuss.

Cougar You're doing it on purpose.

Captain Stop squirming.

Cougar You're only jealous.

Captain Don't say it, Cougar.

Cougar Ouch! There you go again. What is this? The baldy's revenge?

Captain Please, Cougar.

Cougar You must walk round with a pair of tweezers in your pocket. Then, when you see a man with a healthy head of hair, on a bus or something, or when you're walking through the park, or in your junk shop – Sorry! *Antique* shop! You creep up behind them and pluck out a few hairs.

Captain Don't keep on, Cougar. It's not funny. It's hurtful.

Cougar You should set up your own little society. You know, the Bald Phantom Hair Pluckers or something like that. You get together once a month – when the moon is full, or something – and compare how many hairs you've managed to pluck.

Captain I'm not laughing.

Cougar Well, I am! It's hilarious! I can imagine it now. When . . . when you become a member you're given – not a comb – but a piece of cloth and some polish and . . . and you all sit there having skin-polishing contests.

Captain slams tweezers on table and walks away.

Captain Do it yourself! I can't take it any more. All the little jibes and jokes. Upsetting me for no reason. After I've been running around to get things ready for your birthday party as well. Getting the cake. Everything. And what thanks do I get? None. Well, I've had it up to the back teeth. Hear me? Back teeth.

Pause.

I'm going to dust a baby.

Captain gets a china bird and starts dusting it.

Cougar Captain . . .

Captain I'm dusting!

Pause.

Cougar I'm sorry, Captain.

Captain Too late. You think you can just say you're sorry and everything will be forgiven Well, you've gone too far this time.

Pause.

Cougar Is it over then, Captain?

Captain Yes.

Cougar No more larks, Captain?

Captain No more larks.

Cougar You don't mean it, Captain.

Captain I most certainly do.

Cougar But what will Cougar do without his Captain?

Captain You should have thought of that earlier.

Cougar But you know I'm always on pins on my birthday party nights. You know what I'm like, don't you, Captain? You know I'm on pins.

Captain I know.

Cougar And you know I've asked you – asked you millions of times, Captain – to make allowances when I'm on pins. But you don't. You just get in a tizz.

Captain I am not in a tizz.

Cougar When I'm so happy and everything was going so well. I was looking forward to the party. And afterwards we would have talked and had a hug and I would have said, 'Let's have some larks,' or words to that effect. But you have to spoil it all by getting into a tizz just because I'm on pins.

Pause.

Captain Cougar . . .

Cougar Well, if it's over then it's over. If the Captain doesn't want his Cougar then I best pack my bags and clear off.

Cougar stands.

Captain I'm sorry, Cougar.

Cougar No you're not. You're still in a tizz.

Captain I'm not in a tizz.

Cougar You know I'm on pins.

Captain I know. And I am sorry. Don't go. Please sit down. Let me finish plucking your hair.

Cougar No more palaver?

Captain No more palaver.

Cougar Apology accepted.

Cougar sits.

Captain Can I give you a hug?

Cougar If you have to.

Captain approaches Cougar.

Cougar Put your gloves on, though.

Captain puts gloves on.

Cougar You see, it's all too much for me, Captain. You getting into a tizz. It puts my head in a bloody spin.

Captain hugs Cougar.

Captain I'm sorry. It won't happen again.

Cougar That's enough hugging.

Captain A moment longer.

Cougar I'm getting all claustrophobic, Captain.

Cougar pushes Captain away.

Pause.

Cougar Did you like the hug?

Captain Very much.

Cougar hands Captain tweezers.

Captain resumes looking for grey hairs.

Cougar Anyway, I ain't the only one.

Captain The only one what?

Cougar Who's had enough of the birds.

Captain Oh, don't start that again.

Cougar No, listen, Captain. Cheetah Bee's had enough as well. She's had men in.

Captain What men?

Cougar Two of them. They were here today. In white overalls. They're going to . . . to . . .

Cougar can't think of the word. He waits for Captain to supply it.

Captain Exterminate?

Cougar That's it. Exterminate the birds.

Captain But that's terrible.

Cougar Why?

Captain When are they going to do it?

Cougar How should I know? But you want to know an interesting fact?

Captain What?

Cougar I went to school with one of the men. Can you believe that? I tell you, Captain, time has not been kind to him. Receding hair line. Skin all pasty and wrinkled. Bags under his eyes. Double chin. Hairs hanging from his nostrils and sticking out his ears. And as for his body. Christ Almighty. Don't know if I can still call it a body. Fat. Shapeless. Round shoulders. He came up here and he was wheezing like a geriatric. Said to me, 'Cougar,' he said, 'you look just the same as the day you were expelled.' I thought, Wish I could say the same for you, old son. Old being the operative word. Ouch! Thought you said there were only a few.

Captain You want me to get all of them, don't you?

Pause.

Cougar He had his son with him. His son's helping him. We went over the park.

Captain All three of you?

Cougar Just me and the son.

Captain What did you do?

Cougar Had a banana split.

Captain You shouldn't eat ice cream.

Cougar Not getting fat, am I?

Captain It's not good for your insides.

Cougar Who gives a fuck about my insides? Can have a gut full of maggots for all I care, so long as I've got a suntan.

Pause.

Captain So . . . how old is he?

Cougar Who?

Captain The son.

Cougar Didn't ask.

Captain Can't be any more than fourteen.

Cougar Younger, I think.

Captain Has he got nice hair?

Cougar A little short.

Captain So you suggested he grow it? Style it into a quiff?

Cougar How d'you guess?

Captain And he already thinks you're the most exciting person he's ever met.

Cougar Don't they all, Captain . . .? Ahhh! What you trying to do? Scalp me?

Captain All finished.

Cougar Took you long enough.

Captain puts gloves and tweezers away.

Captain You best get ready for the party, Cougar.

Cougar goes to bedroom.

Captain puts sunlamp in corner. It flashes violently a few times. Then he puts tablecloth on table.

Cougar speaks from bedroom.

Cougar Have we got everything, Captain?

Captain Everything.

Cougar The vodka?

Captain Yes.

Cougar Because he only drinks vodka.

Captain I got a bottle.

Cougar Just one bottle?

Captain It'll be enough. I'm not going to drink. I told you.

Cougar What mixer did you get?

Captain Orange juice.

Cougar Orange juice!

Captain It's what you told me to get!

Cougar comes out of bedroom. He is now wearing white T-shirt, black leather jacket , faded denim jeans and black leather boots and sunglasses. His hair is now styled into an impeccable quiff. He is splashing on some aftershave.

Cougar Smell me.

Captain What?

Cougar Come on. Have a whiff.

Captain sniffs.

Captain Good Lord! It's strong. What is it?

Cougar shows Captain the bottle.

Captain Expensive stuff. Nice to know my money's being spent wisely.

Cougar puts bottle on sideboard.

Cougar I'm wearing it for a purpose.

Captain What sort of purpose?

Cougar On purpose.

  Pause.

What about the birthday cards?

Captain Oh . . . yes. Of course.

  Captain gets cards from drawer.

Cougar You get any new ones?

Captain No. We can use the ones from last time.

Cougar How many are there?

Captain Seven.

Cougar Who they from again?

  *Cougar looks in mirror, takes comb from pocket and
  combs his already perfect hair.*

Captain Caroline, Natasha, Sharon, Emma, Shirley,
Clare and Lesley.

Cougar All girls?

Captain That's what we had before. Anyway, Lesley
could be a boy.

Cougar But he'll assume it's a girl. I've told him I've got
lots of male friends as well. Everyone likes me. Not just
girls. I'm popular, Captain. Popular.

Captain Well, we haven't got any new cards.

Cougar You'll have to think of something, Captain.
I want to have male friends as well. Hear me? Male
friends. Mates. Mates.

  Pause.

Captain Perhaps we should make a few of the cards from both a boy and girl. As if they've been sent by a couple.

Cougar Knew you'd think of something.

Captain starts amending cards.

Captain Emma and . . . Steven?

Cougar Nah. Emma and Rod.

Captain Shirley and . . . ?

Cougar Malcolm.

Captain Sharon and . . . Tony?

Cougar Yeah. Tony. Perfect.

Captain That should be enough. Happy now?

Cougar Happy now.

Captain gets cake out of box and puts it on table.

Cougar We should still get some more cards just for male friends. Cards from Russell and Danny and Matt and Sean . . . Names like that.

Captain Come and look at the cake, Cougar.

Cougar looks at cake.

Captain They did us proud this time. Isn't it delectable?

Cougar If you say so.

Captain But look at all that icing, Cougar. The white against the blue.

Cougar Don't know why you're so bothered. You ain't eating any.

Captain I can still look at it.

Cougar You're supposed to eat it, Captain. That's why it's made of yummy things and not sawdust.

Captain I get more enjoyment from looking at it than you get from consuming it.

Cougar I very much doubt it.

Captain That's because you have no aesthetics.

Cougar Fuck aesthetics. Just stick the candles in and hide it in the bedroom. It's supposed to be a surprise. He likes surprises.

Captain Don't refer to him as he. Say his name.

Cougar I forget his name.

Captain No you don't.

Pause.

Cougar Foxtrot.

Captain Foxtrot what?

Cougar Foxtrot Darling.

Captain Oh, what an enchanting name!

Cougar glares at Captain.

Long pause.

Captain I'll . . . I'll get the candles.

Captain goes to cupboard, gets candles, then returns to table.

Cougar continues to glare at Captain.

Captain How many candles shall I put in, Cougar?

Cougar just stares.

Pause.

Captain All nineteen?

Cougar just stares.

Pause.

Captain You're right. All nineteen. Same as always. After all, it is your nineteenth birthday party.

Captain starts sticking candles into birthday cake.

Pause.

Cougar I don't need to know his name to do what I'm going to do to him.

Pause.

Captain I . . . I know, Cougar.

Pause.

Cougar No need for gloves where he's concerned.

Captain Don't . . . please.

Captain stops sticking candles in cake. There is one remaining.

Pause.

Cougar Stick the last candle in, then.

Pause.

Cougar Stick it in.

Captain doesn't move.

Cougar Stick. It. In.

Cougar takes candle from Captain's hand and – with an orgasmic moan – thrusts candle into cake.

Cougar Got to do everything myself now, have I?

Captain I'm sorry.

Cougar You take things too seriously. That's your problem.

Captain I take you seriously. I have feelings for you.

Cougar Then don't. Life's too short to have feelings for people.

Captain Don't you have feelings for me?

Cougar I need you, Captain.

Captain Just need?

Cougar Now don't get all agitated.

Captain I'm not getting all agitated. I'm only asking.

Cougar But you've asked it all before. The same old questions. Over and over again. What good does it do? I need you. Full stop. End of discussion.

Pause.

Captain picks up cake.

Captain I'll hide this so I can surprise you with it later.

Captain takes cake into bedroom.

Cougar Larks, Captain! Don't forget we have our larks!

Captain enters from bedroom.

Captain I can feel one building up, Cougar!

Cougar No, Captain. Don't!

Captain moves towards window.

Cougar tries to stop him.

Cougar You'll just disturb the birds.

Captain If I don't do it, I'm going to explode.

Cougar I don't want screaming birds when he gets here.

They struggle together.

Captain Don't hinder me, Cougar.

Cougar You know, you're stronger than you look.

Captain I'll leak on you!

Cougar backs away.

Captain goes to window and opens it. He sticks his head out and screams. The sound of birds squalling begins. It is piercingly loud!

Cougar There! You've done it now!

Captain faces Cougar.

Captain Good Lord! Listen to them, Cougar!

Cougar Ain't got a fucking choice!

Captain Fly! Fly!

Cougar They'll be shitting everywhere!

Captain Oh, to fly with them, Cougar! To fly and make sounds like that!

Captain starts to move round room, flapping his arms.

Cougar laughs.

Captain To fly through the clouds –

Cougar (*overlapping*) One of these days –

Captain (*overlapping*) – and scream and scream –

Cougar (*overlapping*) – men in white coats –

Captain (*overlapping*) – and not belong to anything –

Cougar (*overlapping*) – will come and take you away.

Captain (*overlapping*) – or anyone –

Cougar (*overlapping*) They'll put you in a funny farm.

Captain (*overlapping*) – and just be free. Free!

Cougar Not much fucking freedom there.

Captain Fly! Fly! Fly!

Cougar shuts window and pulls curtain.

Captain collapses on sofa, giddy.

Cougar You'll make yourself sick, you will.

The birds are getting quieter.

Captain They're calming now! Back to your nests!

Cougar I'll give you back to your fucking nests. What if they'd carried on like that all bloody night? What kind of party would I have had then?

Captain They're calming, Cougar. Don't worry.

Cougar You're a silly old sod sometimes, Captain. Really you are.

Cougar and Captain lean against each other listening to the sound of the birds gradually fade.

Pause.

Captain I have this memory, Cougar. Of what it was like. Perhaps it was only for a week. Or day. Near the beginning of . . . us. A moment when you gave me something. Remember that, Cougar? The Fastest Clock in the Universe. You gave it to me once. Will you ever give it to me again? The Fastest Clock in the Universe.

Long pause.

Suddenly, something hits the window from outside.

Captain Good Lord!

Cougar Christ Almighty!

Captain stands.

Captain It's a bird, Cougar!

Cougar Forget it.

Captain walks toward window.

Cougar Leave it.

Captain It might be injured.

Cougar There's fuck-all we can do.

Captain We can nurse it.

Cougar Leave it, Captain! Come on. Let's choose a magazine for the party. You know how it makes you giggle.

Cougar opens cupboard. It is full of pornographic magazines.

Cougar Come and help me, Captain.

Captain I shouldn't have screamed.

Cougar Look at the pictures. You know they make you giggle. Come on.

Captain is at window.

Cougar Have a fucking giggle, Captain!

Pause.

Captain faces Cougar.

Captain What?

Cougar holds magazine in air.

Cougar Giggle!

Captain Good Lord! Yes, I'm sorry, Cougar.

Slowly Captain goes over to Cougar.

They spread some magazines on floor and start sorting through them.

Captain What does . . . Foxtrot like?

Cougar Women with women.

Captain Lesbians.

Cougar The very same. Find me a good one, Captain. Lots of tongues up pussies and stuff . . . Christ Almighty! Some of these magazines go back to when I was twelve. That's how old I was when I got my first magazine. Me and my best friend stole it. We went to the block of flats where my mate lived and rushed up to the roof. We sat amongst the television aerials and looked at the photographs. I had an erection so hard it hurt. I persuaded my mate to get his cock out. I got mine out too. We played with each other. And then . . . then I got this feeling somewhere in my gut. Like a tiny explosion. And I spunked. It was my first ejaculation. I never dreamed a body could feel something like that. Christ Almighty! I'll never forget it. Sitting up there. Amongst all those television aerials. Somehow, I felt like I was part of an electric current. Every nerve in my body was transmitting particles of sex. My brain sparkled. My hair stood on end. Blood simmered. I imagined myself glowing. A halo of lust buzzing round me. The first real moment of my fucking life.

Long pause.

Captain hands Cougar magazine.

Captain Lesbians.

Cougar looks at magazine.

Cougar Perfect.

Cougar goes to sofa.

Cougar Put the magazines away, Captain.

Cougar hides magazine under sofa.

Captain starts to put magazines back in cupboard.

Cougar practises sitting on sofa and reaching below to produce magazine from under sofa in one swift movement.

Captain begins flicking through magazine.

Captain I don't know what it is about the sight of skin that makes me weep.

Cougar looks at Captain.

Pause.

Cougar Come on, slowcoach. We've got to get things ready.

Captain Oh . . . yes. Of course.

Captain puts remaining magazines in cupboard.

Cougar Now, you know what to do, don't you, Captain?

Captain Same as all the other parties, I suppose.

Cougar We'll let him in.

Captain I know, Cougar. I know.

Cougar Have a few drinks.

Captain That's why I bought the vodka.

Cougar Tell him how popular I am.

Captain Thousands of girlfriends.

Cougar They follow me everywhere.

Captain Like flies.

Cougar And all the time you're . . .?

Captain Pouring vodka.

Cougar Not too much. Don't want him to pass out.

Captain Just tipsy.

Cougar Then I'll give you the signal to leave.

Captain And I'll go. Farewell, Foxtrot Darling.

Cougar And the signal is?

Captain What?

Cougar What's the signal for you to leave the party?

Captain Good Lord! What is this? A test now?

Cougar Just tell me, Captain. I don't want any cock-ups tonight.

Captain I thought that's precisely what you wanted.

Cougar Eh?

Captain Oh, never mind.

Cougar Just tell me the signal for you to leave the party, for chrissakes.

Captain You'll say, 'Isn't it time for your meeting, Captain?'

Cougar And you'll say?

Captain 'Good Lord, yes, Cougar! Thank you for reminding me!'

Cougar And you'll disappear.

Captain I'll have to walk the streets again, I suppose.

Cougar By the time you get back, he'll be gone.

Captain And you'll never want to see him again.

Cougar Why the fuck would I want to see him again?

Captain stares at Cougar.

Pause.

Captain Oh, Cougar.

Pause.

Cougar I ain't told you how I met him yet. And you've got to know, Captain. There's an extra bit this time.

Captain What extra bit?

Cougar A sort of . . . trap.

Captain starts putting knives, forks, plates, glasses, etc. on table.

Captain Trap? Good Lord! What now?

Cougar Listen. I was sunbathing in the park when . . . there he was. Walking very fast and holding some flowers. I was going to follow him then, but I couldn't get my boots on quick enough. You would have laughed.

Pause.

The next day I saw him again. Walking just as fast as before and holding some more flowers. But, again, I couldn't get my bloody boots on in time. So the following day, guess what I did?

Captain I'm all ears.

Cougar Didn't take my boots off! Ha! Good thinking, eh, Captain? This time, when I saw him, I was ready. I followed him. I really liked the way he walked. And his arse looked so fucking –

Captain All right, all right.

Cougar Then I saw where he was heading. The hospital. That's what the flowers were for. He was visiting someone sick. So I followed him into the hospital.

Captain You hate hospitals.

Cougar Shows you how much I wanted him. He went into a ward. I was going to follow him in there too, but a nurse stopped me. So I waited outside. When he eventually came out, he wasn't holding any flowers. But he was with a girl. She was clutching his arm. His girl-friend, I thought. I wanted to smash her fucking face in.

Captain Temper, temper.

Cougar I couldn't help it, Captain. He was so . . . perfect. That slag didn't deserve him. And that night I couldn't stop thinking about him. He was driving me mad – Oh, the table's coming along nicely, Captain.

Captain I'm doing my best. So you went back to the hospital?

Cougar Very next day. Waited outside the ward. He turned up with some flowers and went inside. But this time he came out alone.

Captain Your moment to pounce.

Cougar Exactly.

Captain So who was he visiting?

Cougar His dying brother.

Captain What was he dying of?

Cougar Oh, something terminal. And the girl, Captain – that floozie – she was his brother's girlfriend. Not his. And then a plan stared taking shape in my brain. The perfect trap.

Captain has finished setting the table.

Captain There! All finished!

Cougar Sit down, Captain.

Captain How does it look?

Cougar Fine. Just sit down.

Captain You could show a little appreciation.

Cougar I said it looks fucking fine. What more d'you want? A medal? Now sit the fuck down.

Pause.
Captain sits.

Cougar I've got to tell you about the trap.

Pause.

Captain So? What was 'the trap'?

Pause.

Cougar Savannah Glass.

Captain Savannah Glass?

Cougar My wife.

Captain Your *what*?

Cougar My dying wife. My poor dying wife who was in the same hospital as his poor dying brother.

Captain Oh, no, Cougar.

Cougar What's wrong?

Captain I know you're not exactly the milk of human kindness, but not even you can be so cruel.

Cougar Don't make a song and dance out of it.

Captain To play with the boy's feelings like that. To manipulate him so callously.

Cougar But it's such a perfect lie, Captain. You see, it meant I didn't have to meet the dying brother's floozie either. I simply said I was too upset to meet other girls. And me and him – we became united in grief. Oh, come on. Credit where credit's due.

Captain It's toying with someone's grief!

Cougar Exactly!

Captain But it's monstrous! To simply invent a wife for yourself so you can have your way with the poor, grieving –

Cougar I comforted him, Captain! Put my arm round him. Said I understood when he needed someone to understand. We suffered together. Sometimes he cried when I held him. Have you any idea what a buzz that is? And guess what, Captain. His brother and my wife – what a coincidence! – they died on the same day.

Captain stands.

Captain I won't be part of it.

Cougar You're already part of it!

Captain I'm not. I'll go before Foxtrot gets here. It's too much, Cougar. Even for you. It's too heartless.

Cougar Oh, boo-hoo.

Captain It's diabolical!

Cougar Spoil-sport!

Captain Cannibal!

Cougar Cannibal!?

Captain Yes! Cannibal!

Cougar Christ Almighty! The words you come up with.

Captain To treat the boy like that is just –

Cougar He's not a boy.

Captain How old is he?

Cougar Fifteen.

Captain He's a boy!

Cougar He's not. He can get a hard-on. He can spunk. He's a man, for fuck's sake.

Captain He's a boy and you've used him abominably.

Cougar I gave him what he wanted. A new big brother with a shoulder to cry on. So don't get all righteous with me. We're all as bad as each other. All hungry little cannibals at our own cannibal party. So fuck the milk of human kindness and welcome to the abattoir!

Long pause.

Captain It's about time you grew up.

Cougar Careful, Captain.

Captain All these endless nineteenth birthday parties.

Cougar You'll say something you'll regret.

Captain You can't be a teenager all you life.

Cougar Don't say it!

Captain You've got to accept your age.

Cougar starts clutching at his head in pain.

150

Cougar Don't. Don't, Captain.

Cougar continues to clutch at his head.

Pause.

Captain . . . Cougar?

Cougar It's hurting, Captain!

Captain But . . . but I didn't *say* your age, Cougar.

Cougar Hurting!

Captain Keep in control, Cougar. Don't get violent.
Please. Listen to me. I did not say your age.

Pause.

Shall I get you a drink?

Cougar No.

Captain A cigarette? Would that help?

Cougar Get Cheetah Bee.

Captain Cheetah Bee? Oh, it can't be as bad as that,
Cougar, surely!

Cougar Get her, Captain. Quick!

*Cougar falls to his knees. He is whimpering. His sun-
glasses fall off.*

Captain rushes out of room and down corridor.

Captain Cheetah Bee! Cheetah Bee!

Knocks on door at end of corridor.

Cheetah Bee! It's Captain Tock!

*Cheetah Bee opens door. She is eighty years old, very
wrinkled and virtually toothless. She is wearing a long
brown fur coat and walks with the aid of a walking-
frame.*

Cheetah What's all the hubbub?

Captain Forgive me, Cheetah Bee. But I'm afraid it's Cougar.

Cheetah Oh, not again, Captain.

Cheetah Bee starts to make her way down corridor.

Captain hovers beside her, edging her on.

Cheetah Don't pull me, Captain.

Captain I'm sorry.

Cheetah I can only go so fast, you know.

Captain Of course you can. It's just that it's a special night for Cougar.

Cheetah Another party?

Captain Another party.

Captain and Cheetah Bee enter room and approach Cougar.

Captain Just look at him, Cheetah Bee. What did I tell you?

Cougar's whimpering is getting louder.

Cheetah Bee stands in front of Cougar.

Pause.

Cheetah Look at me, young man!

Cougar goes quiet but does not look up.

Pause.

Cheetah Look at me, I said!

Slowly, Cougar looks.

Cheetah Look at my skin. It is wrinkled and pale. Your skin is tanned and smooth. Why? Because I am at the end and you are at the beginning. Look at my hair. It is colourless and thin. Your hair is black and thick. Why? Because I am at the end and you are at the beginning.

Cougar begins to calm down.

Captain It's working again, Cheetah Bee.

Cheetah It always does.

Captain Carry on. Please. Look at my eyes.

Cheetah Look at my eyes! My vision is fading. Eyes bloodshot and plagued by cataracts. I've stopped producing tears to ease the pain. Whereas your vision is faultless, eyes clear and bright, watering at will. Why? Because I am at the end and you are at the beginning.

Captain (*in unison with Cheetah*) Because she is at the end and you are at the beginning.

Cheetah And my teeth! What few I have are brown and rotten. I can only suck my food and my breath smells of decay. Whereas you have a full head of strong, white teeth and your breath is odourless, inviting kisses. Why? Because I am at the end and you are at the beginning.

Captain (*in unison with Cheetah*) Because she is at the end and you are at the beginning.

Cheetah Everything about me is ruined and faded. I cannot hear properly, walk properly, and all I have before me is sickness and death. But you, everything about you, my stripling, is youthful and perfect. Your hearing is impeccable. You have the agility of an athlete. And you have nothing ahead of you but time, time, time. And why? Because I am at the end and you are at the beginning. I am at the end and you are at the beginning.

Captain (*in unison*) Because she is at the end and you are at the beginning. Because she is at the end and you are at the beginning.

Cougar is calm now.

Pause.

Captain Another success, Cheetah Bee.

Cheetah Sweet Jesus!

Cheetah Bee sits.

Captain Come and sit down, Cougar.

Captain helps Cougar to sofa.

Cheetah Hungry work.

Captain What? Oh . . . yes. Of course. Can I get you something, Cheetah Bee? For all your trouble.

Cheetah That's very generous of you. I am about to cook my tea.

Captain What might tickle your fancy?

Cheetah Have you got any red meat?

Captain I believe I have.

Captain goes to fridge.

Captain gets some liver wrapped in silver foil and takes it to Cheetah Bee.

Captain Liver.

Cheetah Ah, liver is it! In that case I shall make my very special gravy. I make it with vinegar and flour. Very thick and tangy. Let me see . . .

Cheetah begins to open paper.

Cougar moans.

Captain Why don't you lie down for a while, Cougar? You want to be well for your guest. He should be here any minute now.

Captain leads Cougar to bedroom.

Captain It's the liver, Cheetah Bee. He's got such a weak stomach.

Captain and Cougar go into bedroom.

Cheetah He's too squeamish, that's his trouble. The last thing you can be when you watch as much television as I do is squeamish. They're apt to surprise you with a documentary on amputees at any minute.

Captain enters from bedroom.

Cheetah Captain, he turns into a wild animal when you say his age. You should have learnt your lesson by now.

Captain But I didn't say it.

Cheetah Then you threatened to.

Slight pause.

I don't want any more violence.

Captain There won't be any more violence.

Pause.

Cougar told me you had the exterminators for the birds.

Cheetah Oh, it has to be done, Captain. They're rotting everything. I tell you, when I first moved here with my husband – God rest his soul – I thought I was the luckiest girl in the world. Making fur coats was considered glamorous then. And my husband, he made the best. The day we were married he gave me this mink. I was the envy of the street. We came to live here. Above the factory. I got such a thrill every time I walked under the name of the place, 'Immaculate Fur'. One day, I asked him why it was called that. And he said, 'Just look at that coat you're wearing.' I did. But was none the wiser. He didn't say any more. And I felt I shouldn't ask. But, before long, curiosity got the better of me and I went downstairs to see how the animals were killed.

Pause.

Captain And . . . how were they killed?

Cougar (*from bedroom*) Captain!

Captain He's calling.

Captain goes into bedroom.

Pause.

Captain comes out of bedroom.

Captain He wants his sunglasses!

Cheetah Sweet Jesus!

Captain And the mirror!

Cheetah Hallelujah!

Captain starts to collect things together.

Captain He's on the mend, Cheetah Bee, and it's all thanks to you.

Captain goes into bedroom.

Pause.

Foxtrot Darling comes up stairs at end of corridor. He is fifteen years old, hair black and styled in a quiff, pale-skinned, with fragile good looks. He is wearing a school uniform: black blazer, with badge on pocket; grey flannel trousers; black shoes; white shirt and school tie. He is holding a birthday present wrapped in silver wrapping paper.

Foxtrot walks down corridor and nervously enters room.

Foxtrot Hello. Am I on time?

Cheetah Who are you?

Foxtrot Foxtrot Darling. Am I in the right place?

Cheetah Have you got a quiff?

Foxtrot Yeah.

Cheetah Then you're in the right place.

Foxtrot Oh, good. I brought a present. Is that your present?

Cheetah Where?

Foxtrot In your lap.

Cheetah No. It's red meat.

Foxtrot You're kidding. Are you cooking at the party?

Cheetah I'm not invited to the party.

Foxtrot Oh, God. I'm sorry. I thought . . . I mean, I was only . . . Is Cougar here?

Cheetah He's in there. With the Captain. They'll both be out in a tick.

Foxtrot I ain't met the Captain yet. I've heard a lot about him, though. Captain Tock. Captain Tock out in a tick.

Captain comes out of bedroom.

Captain He's going to be just fine, Cheetah Bee.

Captain sees Foxtrot.

Good Lord!

Foxtrot I ain't early, am I?

Captain Foxtrot.

Foxtrot That's right, Captain Tock.

Captain Good Lord!

Pause.

Cheetah stands.

Cheetah Time I was going.

Walks towards door.

There's a programme on television tonight. About a boy born in a jungle. Some place, some time. Born without a face. He's adopted by a surgeon who performs endless operations on him. Gradually, the boy gets a nose, a mouth, ears, eyes. Now he can go to school and do all the things other children do: inject himself with chemicals, watch pornography, arm himself with razor blades, get drunk, get old, wither, die. Sometimes I wonder if it's worth having a face at all.

Cheetah exits.

Captain closes door behind her.

Captain That was –

Foxtrot Cheetah Bee. Your landlady. Eighty years old. Her husband owned the factory below. And now it's full of birds.

Captain We were just talking about that very thing.

Foxtrot And all the knick-knacks in this room are yours.

Captain They're antiques!

Foxtrot Oh, God! Sorry. Antiques. All these antiques are yours. You get them from the junk shop where you –

Captain Antique shop!

Foxtrot Sorry. Antique shop.

Pause.

You've been collecting them for years.

Captain Since before you were born.

Foxtrot You call them your babies.

Captain And they are. My babies.

Foxtrot And dust them all once a day.

Captain Good Lord! Is there anything you don't know?

Foxtrot Don't think so. I feel as if I'm part of this world already. Cougar was right. It is like living inside a huge cracked egg.

Captain I said that. They're my words, not Cougar's.

Pause.

Foxtrot He ain't ill, is he?

Captain No. He's combing his hair.

Foxtrot I've had my hair done the way Cougar likes it.

Captain So I see.

Foxtrot D'you think he'll be pleased?

Captain He'll be over the moon.

Foxtrot I don't look funny?

Captain It suits you.

Foxtrot In my school uniform, I mean. It's a bit small. Weren't time to change.

Captain It looks absolutely fine.

Foxtrot Am I the first one here?

Captain The first and only.

Foxtrot You're kidding! Oh, God . . . I didn't realise it would just be me . . . I hope I ain't made a mistake . . .

Captain Mistake?

Foxtrot goes to sit on sofa. Then stops –

Foxtrot I was going to sit down. Is that all right? It's rude to do it without being asked or something, ain't it?

Captain No, please. Sit.

Foxtrot sits.

Foxtrot Don't want to do anything to upset Cougar, you see.

Captain Of course.

Foxtrot It's just that . . . He did say tonight would be the end of our grieving.

Pause.

You know about my brother, don't you?

Captain Yes. I'm so very sorry.

Foxtrot Did Cougar tell you today would have been my brother's birthday as well?

Captain No. He omitted that one.

Foxtrot Cougar says a coincidence like that must mean something.

Captain Oh, it means something all right.

Foxtrot And, of course . . . well, we were both going through the same thing. Me with my brother. And Cougar with Savannah. He really loved your sister, didn't he?

Pause.

Captain I'll just let Cougar know you're here.

Foxtrot Don't rush him on my account. Tell him to take his time.

Captain goes into bedroom.

Muffled voices are heard in heated argument.

Captain comes out of bedroom.

Foxtrot Nothing wrong, is it?

Captain Nothing at all.

Foxtrot You didn't mention my hair, did you? I want it to be a surprise.

Captain No.

Long pause.

Foxtrot My brother used to take ages getting ready, too.

Captain He did?

Foxtrot Oh, yeah. Combing his hair. Ironing his shirt. Putting on aftershave. I wanted to be like him so much. Does that sound stupid? Suppose it does. It's just that I admired everything about him. The way he walked. Talked. How he didn't seem to need anyone. All he needed was a cigarette and a drink and he was happy. I used to have this . . . oh, I don't know. A fantasy or something. D'you want to hear it?

Captain Please.

Foxtrot One night I would go out with my brother. We'd go to a pub where we'd meet a few of his friends and one of them – a girl – hits me. I don't know why. Anyway, my brother turns to his friends and says, 'If you can't accept my fucking brother, then you can all rot in hell.' And he puts his arm round my shoulders and we walk out of the pub. It's a warm summer's night. We go down to the canal and throw pebbles in the water. My brother tells me I'm the most important thing in his life. He holds me. I smell his aftershave. Oh, God! Listen to me prattling on. Suppose you think I'm just a kid. But . . . I wanted this to happen so much. It never did, though. Because, one day, he met Sherbet Gravel.

Captain Sherbet Gravel?

Foxtrot His girlfriend.

Captain Oh, yes. Of course.

Foxtrot She was a bit of . . . Oh, I don't know the word. She was hard. She mixed with a pretty rough lot. She was a . . . a . . .

Captain Delinquent?

Foxtrot Cougar said you used funny words.

Captain Delinquent's not a funny word.

Foxtrot But I suppose she was. Gangs and stuff. You know? She used to make me nervous. Mind you, all girls made me nervous. I'm prattling on again. Just tell me to belt up. Cougar's probably told you all this anyway?

Captain No, he hasn't. Please carry on.

Foxtrot My brother ran away with Sherbet. We didn't see him for ages. He phoned a few times. But that's all. It's as if we didn't exist for him any more. How can someone do that? Just forget about people?

Captain I don't know.

Foxtrot Anyway, one day, while I was alone in the house, there was a knock on the door. It was Sherbet. She said my brother was in trouble and I had to follow her. She led me down endless roads and streets and alleyways. And all the time it was getting darker and darker. She led me into a derelict building. The brickwork was crumbling. There was no light. It smelt of piss and things. There were rats everywhere. It was like she was taking me to . . . to . . .

Captain The Underworld.

Foxtrot There you go with those words again.

Captain What's wrong with them? They're perfectly descriptive.

Foxtrot You're right! That's just what it was like. The Underworld. Sherbet led me into a small sort of room. The room was empty, except for a pile of cardboard in the corner. And in that pile of cardboard was . . . my brother. This must be boring you.

Captain No.

Pause.

Foxtrot My brother was so thin. He tried to say my name when he saw me. But he couldn't. There were red blotches on his skin. Like cigarette burns. But they weren't. And bruises all up his arms. Fuck, I thought he was going to die right there and then. We got him to hospital and . . . and . . .

Captain Don't carry on if you don't want to.

Foxtrot They put tubes up his nose and in his arm. All I kept thinking was, 'Keep breathing . . . Keep breathing.' Because it was as if . . . Oh, God! How can I explain? You see, going to the hospital, holding his hand, talking to him – even if he didn't hear – kept me on this planet. He was my . . . my . . .

Captain Gravity.

Foxtrot That's right. And, one day, he died and that gravity disappeared. I started to float up. Away from his deathbed. Up through the ceiling. It felt so peaceful. There was no feeling. Just a sense of rising higher and higher. Through the stratosphere and out into the darkness. And I would have stayed there too. Were it not for a voice calling me back. And that voice belonged to –

Captain Cougar.

Foxtrot Cougar! From the first time I met him, I knew he was part of me. I wanted to tell him everything about myself. My favourite films. Food. Television programmes. Everything.

Captain Oh, yes, yes.

Foxtrot And I wanted to be with him all the time. Nothing was real until I told Cougar about it.

Captain Oh, I know, yes.

Foxtrot And all the coincidences: his date of birth. His loss of Savannah. Everything meant we were united somehow. He was my . . . my . . .

Captain Your echo.

Foxtrot Fuck! Yes! My echo! I lost one brother, Captain, but I found another.

There are tears in Foxtrot's eyes.

Slowly, Captain takes handkerchief from his pocket. He holds handkerchief out to Foxtrot.

Foxtrot reaches out for handkerchief.

Just as Foxtrot touches it Cougar erupts from bedroom. His hair is back in an impeccable quiff and he's wearing dark glasses again.

Cougar Party time!

Foxtrot Cougar!

Foxtrot and Cougar embrace tightly.

Foxtrot Oh, Cougar!

Holds embrace for while.

Then Foxtrot sniffs.

Foxtrot Cougar! Your aftershave!

Cougar I'm wearing it for us. Us!

Foxtrot He's wearing my brother's favourite aftershave, Captain. For me and him. Us!

Foxtrot and Cougar embrace again.

Pause.

Foxtrot hands Cougar present.

Foxtrot Happy birthday, Cougar.

Cougar A surprise! Didn't I tell you he liked surprises, Captain. A present, no less.

Foxtrot Hope you like it.

Cougar puts present down.

Cougar I'll open it later. After a few drinks. Captain, start pouring. We're going to have a good party tonight.

Foxtrot How do I look?

Cougar Fine. Captain! Drinks!

Foxtrot Ain't you noticed?

Cougar Noticed what?

Foxtrot Anything different?

Long pause.

Captain His hair.

Cougar Your hair! Christ Almighty! Look at your hair!

Foxtrot You like it?

Cougar Course I do. Noticed it as soon as I saw you.

Foxtrot You're kidding! I did it for you! For us! Took a hell of a long time.

Cougar What a mate! One in a million. Where's those drinks, Captain? Us boys are dying of thirst! Right?

Foxtrot Right! There's . . . there's something I've got to tell you, Cougar.

Cougar Pronto, Captain! Pronto!

Foxtrot You remember you said tonight would be our last night of grieving.

Cougar Have you seen the cards?

Captain Here we go.

> *Cougar hands Foxtrot some cards. Foxtrot looks at them.*

Cougar Lots of girls wanted to come. Didn't they, Captain?

Captain Oh, millions.

Cougar But I told them, 'No! Tonight is for just me and my best mate.' Didn't I, Captain?

> *Foxtrot is trying to get a word in.*

Captain Whatever you say.

Cougar Christ Almighty, were they upset. Right, Captain?

Captain Suicidal, I'd say.

Cougar Don't exaggerate, Captain.

Captain Hurling themselves out of windows, they were.

Cougar What's got into you?

Captain Air full of suicidal girls. All screaming, 'I want to go to Cougar's party.'

Cougar I think you best go, Captain. Ain't it time for your meeting?

Captain Oh, didn't you hear? The meeting's cancelled.

Cougar The meeting's what?

Captain Cancelled!

Cougar drops cards and goes to Captain.

Foxtrot picks up cards.

Cougar The meeting's never cancelled. Now just fuck off. I need my buzz!

Captain Your buzz is not going to happen!

Cougar Not going to . . . I'll fucking kill you, Captain. I swear I will.

Captain I am not leaving you alone so you can lead that lamb to the slaughter.

Foxtrot Please, Cougar. Captain. I have to explain something.

Cougar opens door to corridor. He doesn't see Sherbet Gravel standing in doorway.

Sherbet is sixteen years old, with long curly red hair and lots of glamorous make-up. She is wearing a white uniform, stilettos and clutching a handbag covered in pink sequins.

Foxtrot sees Sherbet.

Foxtrot Oh, God!

Captain sees Sherbet.

Cougar I'll skin you alive, Captain.

Captain (*indicating Sherbet*) Cougar!

Cougar turns to see Sherbet.

Sherbet Hello, all!

Foxtrot You were supposed to wait downstairs.

Sherbet I did wait, Babe. Then I got fed up with waiting.

Foxtrot What's the point of making a plan if you don't –?

Sherbet Happy birthday, Cougar!

Pause.

Foxtrot This . . . this is what I've been trying to tell you. Cougar, Captain, this is Sherbet.

Lights flicker off and on.

Sound of crackling electricity.

Sherbet Tell them, Babe.

Foxtrot Sherbet is *my* girlfriend now.

Lights flicker off and on.

Sound of crackling electricity.

Captain Good Lord!

Sherbet Tell them, Babe.

Foxtrot And she's going to have my baby.

Lights flicker off and on.

Sound of crackling electricity.

Captain Good Lord!

Foxtrot And –

Sherbet We're going to be married.

Sherbet holds Foxtrot's hand.

Lights flicker off and on.

Sound of crackling electricity.

Pause.

Sherbet Ain't come at a bad time, have I?

Pause.

Captain Bad time? No, Sherbet. Not at all. Whoever heard the like? You can't imagine how welcome you are. Come in! Stay!

Captain closes door behind Sherbet.

Lights flicker violently now.

Electricity also crackles violently.

Captain Damn these lights! But – Good Lord! What does it matter? We're going to have a party! Who needs light?

Blackout.

Act Two

Darkness.

Captain enters from bedroom holding birthday cake and large knife. All the candles are lit, illuminating the room.

Cougar, Foxtrot and Sherbet are sitting round the table.

Captain (*brightly singing*)
Happy birthday to you . . .

All (*except Cougar*)
Happy birthday to you,
Happy birthday, dear Cougar,
Happy birthday to you.

Sherbet claps enthusiastically.

Foxtrot joins in.

Captain puts cake on table.

Sherbet Fucking hell, what a beautiful cake. It looks so traditional. I love traditional things. Don't I, Babe?

Foxtrot You do, Babe.

Cougar offers Captain some vodka. Captain refuses.

Sherbet I never used to. But now I can't get enough of them.

Cougar offers Sherbet some vodka. Sherbet refuses.

Sherbet No thanks, Cougar. I don't touch poisons now. Do I, Babe?

Foxtrot You don't, Babe.

Sherbet Ah, yes. Traditional things. Cake on birthdays. Eggs at Easter.

Cougar offers Foxtrot some vodka.

Sherbet Babe don't either. Do you, Babe?

Foxtrot I don't, Babe.

Cougar glares at Foxtrot, then starts drinking from bottle.

Sherbet And Christmas! Ooooh, I love everything to do with Christmas. It's time for the family. Getting together, turkey, Christmas pudding, watching television all afternoon – usually a big film, or cartoons – singing Christmas carols, turkey sandwiches. And then New Year: midnight chimes, arm in arm, 'May old acquaintance be forgot' and all that, a few tears, making resolutions. Christmas and New Year are times for the family. I never used to believe that. But I've changed. The past year has taught me a lot. About the value of traditional things.

Cougar burps.

Foxtrot laughs.

Sherbet Manners, Mr Glass. Manners. Don't laugh, Babe.

Foxtrot Sorry, Babe.

Sherbet Babe has still got a few things to learn. But don't worry. I'm teaching him. You know the first thing I taught him? How to propose.

Foxtrot Don't, Babe.

Sherbet Don't be bashful, Babe. We're amongst friends. You know what I made him do? Go down on one knee –

Foxtrot (*softly, overlapping*) Oh, God.

Sherbet (*overlapping*) – and say, 'Please, Miss Gravel, may I have your hand in marriage?' And I said, 'You may.' He's blushing. Look at him. Bless him. But it's the gospel truth. You know what kind of wedding we're going to have?

Captain A traditional one?

Sherbet Bingo! Not a traditional white wedding, mind you. Because it's not traditional for a pregnant woman to walk down the aisle. But a traditional registry office wedding. People will still wear posh clothes and throw confetti, though. Then we'll have a lovely reception. Salmon and cucumber sandwiches, little sausages on sticks and a big cake, three tiers high. Babe and I, we'll hold the knife and cut the cake together. That's supposed to be good luck, I hear.

Captain Oh, it is.

Sherbet And then . . . then, you know what we'll have? Tell them, Babe.

Foxtrot A honeymoon!

Sherbet Somewhere hot! And then we'll settle down in a . . . Babe?

Foxtrot A traditional house.

Sherbet Little garden out front.

Foxtrot Little garden out back.

Sherbet And we'll have a nursery.

Foxtrot Blue if it's a boy.

Sherbet Pink if it's a girl.

Foxtrot And Babe'll do the cooking.

Sherbet Roast beef on Sunday.

Foxtrot Roast potatoes.

Sherbet Yorkshire pudding.

Foxtrot Mustard!

Sherbet And Babe will have a steady job.

Foxtrot Nine to five.

Sherbet While I do the housework.

Foxtrot Bring up baby.

Sherbet Teach it the ABC.

Foxtrot Nursery rhymes.

Sherbet How to count.

Foxtrot Use the toilet.

Sherbet And the value of traditional things!

Foxtrot (*with Sherbet*) Value of traditional things!

Captain Good Lord! I'm breathless just listening to you both!

Sherbet But don't it sound idyllic, Captain?

Captain Absolute heaven.

Pause.

Sherbet Fucking hell! The engagement ring! I ain't shown you the ring! Now, you all know what to do. I hold out me hand and you make suitable 'ooh' and 'ahh' noises. Ready? Here goes!

Shows ring to Captain.

Captain It's divine, Sherbet. Absolutely divine.

Sherbet Very good, Captain. You pass the test with flying colours.

Sherbet shows ring to Cougar.

Cougar doesn't react.

Sherbet Suitable 'oohs' and 'ahhs', if you please.

Cougar still doesn't react.

Sherbet Cougar's a little skimpy in the 'ooh' and 'ahh' department.

Foxtrot Don't you like the ring, Cougar?

Captain He's been in a barbaric mood all evening.

Sherbet Don't make such a fuss, you two. I know what it is. It's those old birthday blues. Nineteen must be one of those birthdays. Just one more year left of being a teenager. Soon you'll be an old man. With responsibilities and the suchlike. I knew it might take something special to get you in the party mood. So I came prepared.

Picks up handbag.

The handbag!

Opens handbag.

In this bag I've got everything we need.

Reaches into handbag.

Slight pause.

Whips hats out of handbag.

Party hats!

Captain Good Lord!

Foxtrot What a surprise!

Sherbet Now there's one for everyone. Here you are, Babe.

Sherbet gives hat to Foxtrot.

Foxtrot It'll mess up my hair.

Sherbet Don't be a fusspot. It's a party. Let yourself go, Babe.

Foxtrot But I did my hair just for Cougar.

Sherbet *I* did your hair, Babe. Came straight round to the salon he did. Do my hair! Do my hair! Anyone would think his life depended on it. Took a hell of a long time. Bless him.

Foxtrot puts hat on.

Sherbet Captain, this one's for you.

Captain Thank you.

Sherbet gives hat to Captain.

Captain puts it on.

Then Sherbet puts a hat on.

Sherbet And this one's for the Birthday Boy.

Sherbet holds hat out to Cougar.

Sherbet Go on! Put it on!

Cougar does not move.

Pause.

Sherbet You know what I think? I think Cougar's a little tiddly. Am I right? That's what you get for drinking straight from the bottle! I know. I'll put the hat on for you.

Foxtrot He doesn't like anyone touching his hair, Babe.

Sherbet Well, if he doesn't like it, he'll stop me.

Starts putting hat on Cougar.

He'll slap me out of the way and say, 'Don't touch my hair.' Won't you, Birthday Boy? You'll slap me so hard my skull will split in two and all my brains will spill out over the floor.

Finishes putting hat on Cougar.

There you are! Oh, look at you! Ha! You know what you look like? A rabbit caught in car headlights. Don't he, Babe?

Foxtrot He does a bit, Babe.

Sherbet and Foxtrot laugh.

Sherbet Captain? Doesn't he?

Captain Yes, yes indeed.

Captain laughs.

Sherbet A rabbit in car headlights. Frozen stiff by the dazzle. Waiting for the car to run it over. Bless him. Oh, well, at least that's eased the atmosphere a little bit, ain't it? I'm feeling quite relaxed now. You, Babe?

Foxtrot Yes, Babe.

Sherbet You best be careful, Captain. If I make myself too much at home, you'll never get rid of me.

Captain You'd be most welcome, Sherbet.

Sherbet Listen to that, Babe!

Foxtrot What?

Sherbet He's flirting with me. Ain't ya, Captain?

Captain Well, I wouldn't say I –

Sherbet You should stand up for me, Babe. Protect my honour. The Captain might want to have his wicked way with me. Right, Captain?

Captain Why not? You're such a ravishing creature.

Sherbet Ravishing! You hear that, Babe? You'd protect me if someone was out to ravish me, wouldn't you?

Foxtrot Well . . . yeah. Goes without saying.

Sherbet Because I'd do the same for you. If anyone was out to ravish you, I'd do anything to protect you. I'd rip out their hearts with my bare hands before they had a chance to pluck a single hair from your head.

Foxtrot Oh, God, Babe.

Sherbet Babe.

Foxtrot and Sherbet embrace and kiss.

Pause.

Cougar grabs knife on table and lifts it in air.

Captain Cougar! No!

Foxtrot and Sherbet jump apart.

Sherbet Fucking hell!

Foxtrot What's going on?

Captain No, Cougar! No!

Pause.

Sherbet The Captain's right, Cougar. You can't cut the cake yet. You've got to blow the candles out first. Right, Captain?

Captain Absolutely.

Sherbet You make a wish, then blow out all the candles. And if you manage to get all the candles out, your wish comes true.

Foxtrot But you have to do it in one breath, Babe.

Sherbet That's right, Babe.

Foxtrot And something else.

Sherbet Something else?

Foxtrot Something you have to do to make your wish come true.

Sherbet Is it traditional?

Foxtrot Very traditional.

Sherbet What can it be? Make a wish. Blow out the candles.

Captain I know! I know!

Sherbet So there really is something else?

Foxtrot Wasn't lying.

Sherbet Didn't say you were lying, Babe. Fucking hell, what can it be?

Pause.

Foxtrot Give up?

Sherbet All right. I give up.

Foxtrot Captain?

Captain Never tell anyone your wish.

Foxtrot That's right! That's right!

Sherbet Fucking hell. Of course. Of all the things to forget.

Foxtrot Well done, Captain.

Sherbet Now, Cougar. You know all the rules. Blow candles out. Use only one breath to do it. And never tell anyone your wish. On the count to three, fill those lungs and give us a tornado! Ready? One . . . Two . . . Three!

Cougar doesn't move. He toys with knife.

Pause.

Sherbet The party hat don't seem to have helped much, does it? Come on, everyone. Let's give him some encouragement. We'll say it together . . .

All (*except Cougar*) One . . . Two . . . Three!

Cougar doesn't move.

Foxtrot Why ain't you making a wish, Cougar?

Pause.

Sherbet I know why. Because he's got everything! Nothing left to wish for. Lucky old Cougar. Right, Babe?

Foxtrot Right, Babe.

Pause.

Sherbet Wish I was lucky enough not to want a wish. What about you, Captain? If you could have one wish, what would it be?

Captain Good Lord! I don't know.

Sherbet But you must have one.

Captain Well . . . yes, I have.

Foxtrot Tell us, Captain.

Captain I don't know if I can.

Sherbet Oh, bless him. You're amongst friends, Captain.

Foxtrot Please, Captain. Please.

Slight pause.

Captain Hair.

Slight pause.

I was eighteen when my hair started to fall out.

Foxtrot Eighteen! You're kidding!

Sherbet Shush, Babe. Go on, Captain.

Captain At first, I thought it was just a phase. I thought it would grow back. I went to see a doctor. He said nothing could be done. My hair would never grow back. I became suicidal. I was going . . . I couldn't even say the word! I still find it difficult. Once I knew it was happening, I became obsessed with hair. Suddenly, everywhere I went people were talking about hair. How they were going to grow it, cut it, bleach it, perm it, dye it, streak it. When I walked down the street, I didn't look at people's faces or what they were wearing. I just looked at their hair. And when I thought of the future, I didn't think, 'By then I'll be doing this,' or, 'By then I'll be doing that.' I just thought, 'By then I'll be . . . bald.' You don't know what it's like the first time someone says, 'You're going bald!' And it's said like an accusation. As if it's something you've done. Your fault in some way. Something deficient in your diet. And then the accusatory tone goes and it's replaced with something worse. Amusement! And they're laughing. They find it funny. Hysterical. All your suicidal thoughts, your nights of tears, your hours counting dead hairs. It doesn't mean anything to them. All they're thinking is, 'Glad it's not me.' And, 'Doesn't he look ugly?'

Pause.

Sherbet But . . . you don't look ugly at all.

Captain Oh, take no notice of me.

Sherbet Captain ain't ugly, is he, Babe?

Foxtrot No.

Sherbet You're beautiful, Captain. A beauty that has fuck-all to do with hair or sun-tan or what you wear. A beauty that will never age. Don't you think so, Cougar?

Pause.

Suddenly Cougar violently blows candles out.

His sudden movement makes Sherbet yelp out loud.

Captain Cougar!

Sherbet Fucking hell!

Foxtrot Oh, God, Cougar! You made me jump!

Sherbet Me, too, I can tell you.

Captain He did it on purpose.

Pause.

Sherbet Well, at least he made a wish, bless him. The hat must be working after all.

Pause.

We haven't got to sit here in the dark, have we, Captain?

Captain Don't panic. There's a candelabrum at the ready.

Foxtrot Captain Tock to the rescue!

Captain goes to candelabrum and starts lighting candles.

Sherbet I love candelabrums. They're so –

Foxtrot Traditional.

Sherbet No, Babe. Romantic. Right, Captain?

Captain lights candelabrum.

Captain Well, it all depends where you are, I suppose.

Pause.

One day I lit this candelabrum and went downstairs to the abandoned factory.

Holds candelabrum aloft.

And I opened a door I had never opened before.

Sherbet Oooh, Captain. I'm gripped already. Did you go inside?

Captain I did. It was very dark. I lifted the candelabrum. And I looked.

Sherbet What can you see?

Captain The universe! I'm floating in space. Around me are millions of stars, all tinged with orange, zodiac after zodiac, all glowing like tiny sparks. And then . . . then I see other things. Things between the stars. Silver things glinting. Tiny hooks. Tiny daggers. Suddenly the universe is not a safe place to be. And the stars begin to move. And . . . and I hear a noise. The noise is all round me. A noise I've never heard before. Strange bird calls . . .

*Sherbet begins to make gentle haunting bird-calls.
Foxtrot follows her lead.*

Captain And then I see. The stars are not stars. They're eyes. Birds' eyes. And the hooks are not hooks. They're claws. And the daggers are beaks. The noise . . . the noise gets louder . . .

The bird-calls from Foxtrot and Sherbet get louder.

Captain Then I begin to see other things. Cages. Knives. Scissors. Electric wire. It's like a torture chamber. I'm in the biggest torture chamber in the universe.

The lights come on.

Foxtrot Light!

Sherbet Bingo! You're dripping wax on the floor, Captain.

Captain Good Lord! Thank you.

Captain blows candles out and puts candelabrum down.

Sherbet Now I can see the place properly!

Sherbet looks round.

You like your birds, don't you, Captain?

Captain They're a bit of an obsession, yes.

Sherbet More than a bit, I'd say. You know what gets me? Their faces. They never show any feeling, do they? I bet you could put a bird through a mangle feet first and the look on its face wouldn't change one jot.

Continues to look round.

Fucking hell, look at the walls. Just like living in – what was it Cougar said, Babe? A huge cracked egg.

Captain That's my expression. I said that.

Sherbet You said Cougar said it, Babe.

Foxtrot I did, but –

Captain He didn't. They're my words. I've been saying them for years.

Sherbet Naughty fibber, Mr Glass.

Foxtrot Perhaps I misheard.

Sherbet Think so, Babe?

Foxtrot Might have, Babe.

Sherbet In that case, I'm sorry, Cougar. I shouldn't have called you a liar. I'm sure you wouldn't have deliberately misled my Babe. Misleading people is a shocking thing to do.

Pause.

Captain Good Lord! Why don't you two tell me your wishes? After all, I've told you mine. What would yours be, Foxtrot?

Foxtrot Oh, God. I don't know. What about you, Babe?

Sherbet Well, in a way I've got everything I could ever wish for in this very room. My future husband. A baby on the way. Good friends. What more can I wish for? But . . . well, but I do I'm ashamed to say.

Foxtrot What, Babe?

Sherbet Tell us yours first, Babe.

Foxtrot No. You, Babe.

Sherbet You, Babe.

Foxtrot You, Babe.

Sherbet You, Babe.

Foxtrot But I don't know. I've never thought about it.

Sherbet Bless him. Think about it.

    Pause.

Foxtrot Whiskers! That's it. Whiskers! I like the idea of coming home drunk at night, falling asleep with my clothes on, and waking up in the morning with stubble. My brother has very thick whiskers. *Had* very thick whiskers. And I like the idea of shaving and putting on lots of aftershave. My brother's favourite. Yeah, that's it. Whiskers! That's my wish.

Sherbet But that ain't a proper wish, Babe.

Foxtrot It is. It's what I want.

Captain What Sherbet is saying is that . . . well, whiskers are bound to happen. It's like wishing for . . . oh, I don't know . . .

Sherbet Wrinkles.

Captain Exactly.

Foxtrot How come?

Sherbet Well, wrinkles are inevitable, Babe. When you wish for something, it should be something that might not be possible.

Foxtrot Some men don't get whiskers.

Sherbet Very few, Babe.

Foxtrot It's possible.

Sherbet But not probable.

Foxtrot What's the difference?

Captain Well, possible means it –

Foxtrot Oh, God! I don't want a bloody argument.

Sherbet We're not arguing, Babe.

Foxtrot You are! It's only a game. Didn't know there was a long list of rules and regulations about making a bloody wish. I wish for whiskers! That's it! Don't want a lecture!

Pause.

Sherbet Who wants to know my wish?

Captain Me, please.

Sherbet Babe?

Foxtrot What?

Sherbet Do you want to know my wish?

Foxtrot All right.

Sherbet All right what?

Foxtrot All right, Babe.

Sherbet I wish to grow old gracefully. Now I know that sounds ridiculous, but I've seen enough people not doing it gracefully to know what I'm talking about. The beauty salon where I work is full of them. Men and women. All with the same look in their eyes. Make me young, says the look. But you know something? There's nothing we can do. Nature has rules and regulations and most of them are either cruel or fucking cruel. You know, I can usually tell a person's age as easy as that! One look is all it takes. Fancy that, Cougar, eh?

Cougar backs away.

Sherbet There's this one woman who comes in – I feel sorry for her in a way – and she's got this photograph of what she looked like when she was nineteen. She must be sixty if she's a bloody day now. Anyway, she comes in and she shows me this photo and – fucking hell! – was she beautiful! 'This was me,' she says. It's as if that photograph captured her at the happiest moment of her life. Perhaps it's like that. Perhaps we reach our peak when we're nineteen and, for one glorious summer, we're in control of our lives, and we look wonderful and everything is perfect. And then it's never the same again. And we spend the rest of our lives merely surviving one empty summer after another.

Captain I . . . I don't think it's like that at all. You might not live that same summer again, but others are glorious for different reasons.

Sherbet I'm sure you're right, Captain. Anyway, I ain't afraid of getting old. It's only natural.

Cougar goes over to sofa.

Captain (*at Cougar*) If you're not in the party mood, why don't you just leave?

Cougar glares at Captain.

Sherbet Ooo, what a look.

Captain He won't go.

Foxtrot Why should he go? It's his party.

Sherbet Grumpy, Mr Glass.

Captain If you can't have your own way, you'll just spoil it for everyone else, won't you!

Sherbet Now, now, now! Let's not make too much of it. You're too hard on him. We're supposed to be having fun and games. But, don't worry, handbag to the rescue!

Holds handbag up.

I told you, I've got everything in here to put us in a party mood.

Puts hand in bag.

Can you guess what I've got this time?

Pause.

No?

Pulls out plastic glasses with false noses attached.

Masks! Well, almost masks. Plastic glasses with noses actually. But they were so funny, I just had to get them. Captain, this one's for you.

Captain Thank you.

Captain puts mask on.

Sherbet Babe, this is for you.

Foxtrot Thanks, Babe.

Foxtrot puts mask on.

Sherbet I said we'd have a good party, didn't I, Babe? One way or another. Ooo, Babe! Look at Captain!

Laughs.

Foxtrot Oh, God! Captain!

Laughs.

Sherbet And look at you, Babe! You look just as funny!

Foxtrot You're kidding! Do I?

Captain Good Lord, yes!

Sherbet Don't make me laugh too much. The Future One will start fluttering.

Puts mask on.

How do I look?

Foxtrot and Captain laugh.

Foxtrot Suits you, Babe.

Sherbet Don't push your luck.

Captain He's right, Sherbet. It does.

Sherbet You're wicked, you two!

Holds out final mask.

And this one is for Birthday Boy.

Takes mask to Cougar.

Foxtrot Put it on, Cougar.

Sherbet Come on, Cougar!

Captain Yes, put it on.

Sherbet Get in the party mood, for fuck's sake.

Cougar doesn't react.

Pause.

Sherbet Shall I put it on for you? Is that what you want? I think it's all the drink. Made him a little numb, bless him.

Pause.

I'll put it on.

Sherbet takes off Cougar's sunglasses.

Cougar stares at Sherbet.

Slowly, Sherbet starts to put mask on Cougar.

Cougar plays with knife.

Sherbet We'll all wear masks. Our faces will be hidden. Who knows what we're thinking? Or what we might do? My, anything could happen. Anything at all.

The mask is on.

Sherbet There! What d'you think?

Sherbet and Foxtrot laugh.

Foxtrot A definite improvement.

Sherbet I think so too. You should keep it on. Then you'll have even more girls after you. I bet all these cards are from your female admirers.

Picks up card.

I was right! Caroline!

Picks up another card.

And this one? Natasha. Oh, yeah.

Looks at more cards.

Yeah! Yeah! Just as I thought. Your little harem. I would have thought they'd be here tonight. Would have been nice for me, if nothing else. To have some girls to natter

189

with. Could have asked them why they all used the same pen to start with. Perhaps they all wrote them together. As a group. I know that's what me and my friends used to do on Valentine's Day. All get together for a mammoth card-writing session. Fucking hell, that was fun. Mind you, I was young then.

Captain Good Lord! You're young now. You can't be more than . . . what? Seventeen?

Sherbet Sixteen! But I'm getting on, Captain. Half way through me teens. Ooo, it must be hell not to be a teenager. Cougar knows what I mean. Only one year left for him. And look, he's hardly a bundle of laughs, is he?

Foxtrot That ain't fair, Babe.

Sherbet What? Oh, I'm sorry, Babe. Of course it's not. Sorry, Cougar. You've been through so much. Losing your poor wife like that. I know what it's like. But you've got to make an effort. It's your birthday. You know . . . Cake! Funny hats! Pres – Fucking hell! The present! You ain't even opened your present yet.

Foxtrot Forgot all about it.

Captain Good Lord! So did I.

Sherbet puts present in Cougar's lap.

Sherbet There you are!

Foxtrot Babe chose it.

Sherbet It was you, Babe.

Foxtrot You really, Babe.

Sherbet Both of us chose it. Now, go on. Open it.

Foxtrot Yeah. Open it.

Pause.

Slowly, Cougar cuts away wrapping paper with knife.

Sherbet Knew that knife would come in handy.

Foxtrot Hope you like it, Cougar.

Foxtrot sits next to Cougar on sofa.

Sherbet Of course he'll like it. Come closer, Captain.

Captain I'm fine just here.

Sherbet No, come closer. You don't want to miss the look on his face when he sees it.

Captain comes closer.

Sherbet Look at him. He can hardly contain his excitement, bless him.

Cougar grudgingly opens present to reveal a clock.

Sherbet There!

Foxtrot A clock!

Captain Good Lord!

Foxtrot D'you like it?

Pause.

Cougar is trembling, clutching the knife.

Foxtrot Say you like it.

Captain Give it to me, Cougar.

Captain gets up and takes clock from Cougar.

Foxtrot You don't like it, do you?

Captain I'm sure he does.

Sherbet Not so much as a thank you.

Captain Gratitude isn't one of his strongest points.

Sherbet That's just bad manners.

Foxtrot I don't think he likes it.

Sherbet He could still say thank you, Babe. Shame on you, Mr Glass! Really! Shame!

Captain I know a story about a clock.

Cougar stares at Captain.

Sherbet Do you? Ooo, I love stories. So do you, don't you, Babe?

Foxtrot Yes, Babe.

Sherbet Tell us the story, Captain.

Cougar glares at Captain.

Captain Good Lord, I . . . I don't know. Perhaps I shouldn't have mentioned it.

Sherbet No, no, no. Tell us! Here. I'll sit down.

Sherbet sits on floor in front of Foxtrot and Cougar.

Sherbet We're your captive audience. Where's the story come from, Captain?

Captain I . . . I made it up.

Foxtrot Oh, God. You're kidding!

Sherbet That does it! You've got to tell us now, Captain. No arguments. Come on!

Pause.

Captain faces them.

Captain I . . . I made this up many years ago. For someone I met. Someone . . . someone I cared for a great deal. Someone who did not care for me.

Sherbet That's the worst thing in the world.

192

Captain Yes, it is. And so . . . this story came into my head. I don't know where it came from. One day it was there, as if it had always been there.

Sherbet Tell us, Captain.

Foxtrot Yeah. Please, Captain.

Pause.

Captain Once, a long time go, there lived the most beautiful Prince in the World –

Cougar yawns loudly.

Slight pause.

Captain Everywhere he went people followed him, content merely to be near him. Every morning the Prince would look at the sunrise and say, 'I am more adored than you, because there are some who burn easily in your light.'

Cougar feigns sleep and starts to snore.

Captain And every night the Prince would look at the stars and say, 'I am more adored than any of you, because there are some who despise the dark that you need to shine.'

Cougar's snoring gets louder.

Sherbet Less noise in the peanut gallery, if you please.

Foxtrot nudges Cougar.

Cougar continues snoring.

Captain And so it went on. The Prince roamed the land, adored by all who saw him. 'How stupid people are,' said the Prince. 'I am their world, yet they mean nothing to me.'

Cougar's snoring gets louder.

Sherbet Fucking hell.

Foxtrot Cougar!

Foxtrot nudges Cougar.

Captain Ignore him! Just . . . ignore him.

Pause.

And then, one day, the Prince met a Wizard. The Prince
told the Wizard how he was adored by everyone and
how funny he found it. Because he cared for no one.
The Wizard said, 'You might be the most beautiful thing
in the world, but you are also the most cruel. Your face
shows no expression. It is hard and emotionless. Like
the face of a vulture. To punish you, I will put a spell
on you.'

Cougar continues snoring.

Captain Quiet, Cougar!

Cougar feigns 'waking up'.

Sherbet You're missing a good story, Cougar. You
shouldn't have drunk so much. Oh, carry on, Captain.
What was the spell? Something fucking nasty, I hope.

*Cougar encourages Foxtrot to take several large swigs
from the vodka bottle as –*

Captain The Wizard changed the Prince's face into the
face of a vulture. His hair fell out and was replaced with
feathers. His nose grew longer and harder and turned
into a beak. The Prince screamed and screamed and
begged the Wizard to give him back his beautiful face.
'No,' said the Wizard. 'The only thing that will save you
is when you find the Fastest Clock in the Universe.'

194

Cougar reaches down and gets the pornographic magazine from under the sofa.

Captain And so the Prince wandered the land. He looked everywhere for the Fastest Clock. But what was it? What did it look like? Was it big or small?

Cougar begins flicking through the magazine. He shows Foxtrot a photograph.

Captain He asked everyone he met. But when they saw his face they ran away, screaming, 'Go back to hell, you vulture!'

Foxtrot starts to get interested in magazine.

Captain Years passed –

Sherbet What a lovely phrase. Years passed. Sorry, Captain.

Cougar turns pages in magazine.

Foxtrot becomes more interested.

Captain One day, while he was looking for food in a forest, the Prince met a girl. The Prince went up to the girl and said, 'I am weak and hungry. Will you help?' And the girl replied, 'Of course.'

Sherbet I bet she was blind.

Captain That's right. The girl was blind.

Sherbet Did the Prince tell the Blind Girl about his search for the Fastest Clock?

Captain Yes, he did.

Sherbet And she knew where to find it?

Captain No. But she said she would help him search. The sound of his crying had touched her heart.

Foxtrot giggles at a photograph.

Sherbet Quiet back there! Where did they search, Captain?

Captain Everywhere. One day, while they were walking through a forest, the Prince's foot got caught in a steel trap. The trap clasped round the Prince's ankle like steel jaws.

Sherbet Fucking hell!

Captain Using all her strength, the Blind Girl tried to open the trap. But she couldn't.

Foxtrot takes another swig from bottle.

Cougar starts to stroke Foxtrot's hair.

Sherbet Get help! Get help!

Captain Oh, she did. She ran through the forest until she found a man chopping down a tree. She asked him to follow her. He did so. But when the man saw the face of the Prince, he screamed.

Foxtrot begins to look at the photographs more intently. The giggles fade away. He is getting more and more turned on.

Cougar removes their masks and hats, then puts his hand on Foxtrot's knee and squeezes.

Sherbet Stupid fucking man!

Captain 'It's a terrible creature,' he said. 'And it deserves to die!' And the man lifted his axe into the air.

Sherbet No!

Cougar begins to feel along Foxtrot's leg.

Foxtrot opens his legs, turns page in magazine.

Captain The Blind Girl shielded the Prince from the axe, shouting at the man, 'I won't let you hurt one feather on his head!'

Cougar's hand is almost on Foxtrot's crotch.

Sherbet Yes! One feather on his head!

Cougar begins rubbing Foxtrot's crotch.

Captain And then . . . the Prince started to change. The feathers and beak disappeared. And he . . . he became the most beautiful thing in the universe again. And . . . and he and the Blind Girl lived together for the rest of their lives.

Cougar loosens Foxtrot's trousers.

Sherbet So the vulture face had gone?

Captain Yes.

Sherbet Oh, beautiful.

Cougar's hand slips into Foxtrot's trousers.

Captain Because at that moment, when they thought they were going to lose each other and they embraced . . . they . . . found . . .

Cougar starts masturbating Foxtrot.

Captain . . . the Fastest Clock in the Universe –

Foxtrot moans gently.

Captain jumps up angrily to his feet.

Captain Stop it! Stop it!

Foxtrot jumps to his feet.

Sherbet looks round.

Foxtrot What's the problem? What?

Hurriedly does up trousers.

Sherbet sees magazine.

Sherbet Fucking hell! You looking at this, Babe?

Foxtrot A little bit.

Sherbet Why?

Foxtrot Cougar showed it to me.

Sherbet You should have moved away.

Captain (*at Cougar*) You won't give up, will you!

Foxtrot It's only a laugh.

Sherbet It's disgusting.

Foxtrot Says who?

Sherbet Says me!

Foxtrot Ooo, the mighty Sherbet has spoken!

Sherbet What's that supposed to mean?

Foxtrot Perhaps I'm fed up with all your fucking
opinions. You thought of that? Perhaps I'm not ready for
all your fucking traditional things and if you don't like it
you can just piss off.

Long pause.

Cougar puts sunglasses back on. He grins at Sherbet.

Slight pause.

Sherbet clutches her stomach.

Sherbet Fucking hell.

Captain What's wrong, Sherbet?

Sherbet It's nothing, Captain.

Captain Sit down.

Captain helps Sherbet sit.

Captain Is it the baby?

Sherbet Don't make a fuss now. The Future One is only moving about. Heard its dad's voice, I reckon.

Captain I think the whole street heard its dad's voice.

Sherbet Ooo, it's kicking. Want to feel, Captain?

Captain Can I?

Sherbet lays Captain's hand on her stomach.

Slight pause.

Sherbet There!

Captain Remarkable.

Sherbet I think Future One wants its dad to feel it. That's what it wants.

Captain Most definitely.

Slight pause.

Sherbet Ooo, another kick.

Slight pause.

Ooo, another kick.

Foxtrot Can I . . . feel it?

Sherbet Didn't think you'd want to. Daddies feeling their Future One is a very traditional thing.

Foxtrot I . . . want to.

Sherbet Put your hand here, then.

Foxtrot lays his hand on Sherbet's stomach.

Slight pause. Then –

Foxtrot gasps and laughs as he feels a kick.

Sherbet strokes his hair and grins at Cougar.

Slight pause.

Sherbet Babe cares so much for the Future One.

Captain I can see that, yes.

Pause.

Sherbet It is his, you know.

Captain Oh, Good Lord, I never thought otherwise.

Sherbet Yes you did. Everyone does. But, believe me, Babe's brother had been too ill to make Future Ones for quite a while.

Pause.

Me and Babe visited Babe's brother in hospital every day. Didn't we, Babe?

Foxtrot Yes, Babe.

Sherbet Babe brought fresh flowers every time. Didn't you, Babe?

Foxtrot Yeah.

Pause.

Sherbet And then, one night, I was walking home from the hospital with Babe – although he wasn't my Babe then, you understand – and I grabbed hold of Babe as tight as I could –

Foxtrot takes his hand from Sherbet's stomach.

Foxtrot Oh, God! This is a bit personal, don't you think?

Sherbet The Captain will understand. We were under a bridge. It was very dark. I grabbed hold of Babe and

200

tore at his clothes. I stripped him naked. Grabbed his arse. Touched him everywhere. He was moaning and groaning. And I fucked him. Right there. Didn't I, Babe?

Slight pause.

Foxtrot nods.

Pause.

Sherbet We've seen it. Ain't we, Babe?

Foxtrot What?

Sherbet The Future One.

Foxtrot Yeah! On a screen.

Captain A screen?

Sherbet A scanner. In hospital.

Foxtrot Millions of spots of light. Like . . . like . . .

Captain Constellations?

Foxtrot Yeah. Constellations.

Captain Constellations of arms.

Foxtrot And legs.

Sherbet And toes.

Captain And the head was like . . . Jupiter?

Sherbet Oh, yes!

Captain And you could see its eyes?

Foxtrot Yeah! Its eyes . . . eyes like . . . like two moons!

Captain And the veins across its skull?

Foxtrot The tails of comets!

Captain Its ears?

Sherbet Craters.

Captain Craters of?

Foxtrot Craters of?

Sherbet Meteors!

Captain Very good!

Sherbet Ancient meteors!

Captain Better still! Bravo, Sherbet.

Captain and Foxtrot applaud.

Sherbet I'm really having a good time!

Foxtrot Me too.

Sherbet Really, Babe?

Foxtrot Really, Babe.

Sherbet and Foxtrot hold hands.

Slight pause.

Cougar doesn't move.

Pause.

Captain I wasn't going to eat any cake. But now . . . now I think I will. The icing looks so tempting. Perhaps I should cut it.

Sherbet Oh, let Cougar cut it, Captain. It's bad luck if anyone else does it.

Captain I know, but I –

Sherbet And fancy thinking you weren't going to have a slice.

Captain I know, I know. But I've got a cupboard full of vitamins over there. It seems ludicrous to take them, then fill my stomach with –

Sherbet It won't hurt you, Captain. Will it, Babe?

Foxtrot Course not, Babe.

Captain But it does weaken one's defences and –

Sherbet Fucking hell! Everyone wants to live for ever these days. And look younger. Vitamins for this. Plastic surgery for that. You wouldn't think immortality and eternal youth would be too much to ask for, would you? But it is! We all get old and drop dead some day. And all the surgery and tablets in the world won't help you one fucking atom.

Pause.

Cougar, I know what you're going through. Believe me. I do. Don't you think I know how guilty you feel about it all? Having a party when you so recently lost your wife. But she's gone, Cougar, and you've got to –

Foxtrot Babe, I don't think –

Sherbet No, Babe. This has to be said. There are certain things we have got to talk about tonight. That's why I'm here.

Removes mask and hat.

I have a secret I want to tell. Something not even my Babe knows.

Foxtrot What, Babe?

Pause.

Sherbet I need my handbag.

Foxtrot gives Sherbet her handbag.

Pause.

Sherbet One day, when I got to the hospital to visit Babe's brother, I saw a man waiting outside the ward. This man was wearing a leather jacket, white T-shirt, blue jeans, boots and his jet-black hair – his badly *dyed* jet-black hair – was styled in a quiff. I thought nothing more of it. Only he was there the next day. And the next.

Foxtrot Babe, what're you –?

Sherbet Shush, Babe!

Pause.

One day, I mentioned this to my Babe. Babe told me that this man was his new friend. His name was Cougar Glass and he was in the hospital because his wife was dying. My Babe told me that Cougar Glass was like a new older brother. And there were so many coincidences that linked them together. Ooo, I wanted to meet this miraculous friend. Because that's what I thought it was. A miracle. But I was told I could not meet him. Why? Because meeting girls reminded him of his dying wife. I asked her name. Savannah Glass.

Pause.

One day I went to the hospital and my Babe's brother was dead.

Pause.

One day, two deaths.

Pause.

Because on that same day – probably at the very same minute for all I know – your sister died, didn't she, Captain?

Captain What? Oh . . . yes, yes.

Sherbet Were you in the hospital?

Captain I . . . I think so.

Sherbet Don't you know?

Captain Yes. I was.

Sherbet Did she suffer?

Captain No.

Sherbet I'm glad.

Pause.

One day, the day after I first heard about Savannah Glass, I asked a nurse where I could find her.

Captain Good Lord!

Foxtrot Babe, I told you not to –

Sherbet I know, I know. But I felt I had to, you see.

Pause.

Sherbet And the nurse took me to a ward. And . . . and this is my secret.

Pause.

I met Savannah Glass.

Captain removes mask and hat.

Captain What's going on here?

Sherbet I introduced myself.

Captain What game are you playing?

Sherbet What game am *I* playing! That's a fucking fine one! Now, listen to me, Captain. I talked to Savannah for ages. She told me a lot of things. What a wonderful creation she was. She told me one thing in particular.

Something I have to mention now! Can you guess what it is? Eh?

Slight pause.

Captain What?

Sherbet Cougar's real age.

Cougar stands.

Captain Good Lord! You don't know what you're doing.

Foxtrot Real age? But he's nineteen.

Sherbet Course he ain't, Babe. I know his fucking type! Hear me, Cougar? I know your tricks! Knew them the first time I clocked you!

Captain Stop it now!

Foxtrot Not nineteen. I don't understand.

Sherbet I can guess your real age, Cougar!

Captain Don't say it! Please. Don't say it.

Sherbet You hear me, Cougar! I know how old you are.

Captain For God's sake don't . . .

Cougar starts to clutch his head and whine.

Foxtrot What's happening? What?

Captain Just go, Sherbet! Please! You don't know what you're doing!

Sherbet I know exactly what I'm fucking doing!

Cougar begins to whine louder. His sunglasses fall to the floor.

Captain Oh! Good Lord! No!

Foxtrot Babe? Cougar? What's this all about?

Captain Don't do anything, Cougar. Please. Keep in control.

Cougar takes a step towards Sherbet, the knife raised to strike.

Captain No! No!

Sherbet takes a gun from her handbag.

Cougar stops.

Foxtrot Babe! Oh, God! What you up to?

Captain Sherbet! Don't say it!

Sherbet Shut up, both of you!

Pause.

Happy thirtieth birthday, Cougar.

Cougar lets out a piercing howl! He hurls himself at Sherbet, knife raised.

Foxtrot lunges at Cougar, restraining the hand with the knife.

Captain rushes to Sherbet, grabbing the hand with gun.

Aimed at the ceiling, the gun fires!

(All this happens in an instant!)

The moment the gun fires . . . all the lights (and the sun-ray lamp) start flickering violently, giving a strobe effect. And the birds start shrieking deafeningly loud. Everything exaggerated to the extreme.

Sherbet is striking at Cougar, Cougar at her.

Foxtrot and Captain are trying to separate them.

Foxtrot Stop it, Cougar! Oh, God.

Captain Don't! Don't! Let go of the gun! Let go before you kill someone.

Sherbet Perhaps I want to fucking kill someone!

They are fighting violently now, Sherbet on the floor striking at both Cougar and Captain.

Cougar is howling and trying to stab Sherbet with his knife.

Foxtrot begins to punch Cougar. Much kicking, hitting and clawing.

Furniture gets knocked over, the tablecloth is pulled to the floor.

Sherbet and Cougar are disarmed.

Cougar picks Sherbet up. He slams her violently on table.

Cougar punches Sherbet in the stomach.

Sherbet screams and kicks.

Cougar continues punching.

Sherbet bleeds profusely between legs.

The blood goes everywhere

Foxtrot Blood!

Sherbet Ahhh! Blood! No! Blood!

Captain (*overlapping*) Blood! Blood! Blood! Blood!

Sherbet (*overlapping*) Blood! Blood! Blood! Blood!

Foxtrot (*overlapping*) Blood! Blood! Blood! Blood!

Cougar backs away from Sherbet and collapses to the floor, pulling curtains with him.

At that precise moment the lights stop flickering and remain out.

Brilliant moonlight illuminates the room.

The shrieking birds remain, but their sound is diminishing.

Foxtrot goes to Cougar.

Foxtrot What's fucking wrong with you? I didn't want this to fucking happen. I didn't want – I could fucking kill you, you crazy fuck!

Captain Foxtrot, don't!

Foxtrot Fucking kill you. Kill you! Kill you!

Captain There's no time for any of that! Just help me. Come on! We'll take Sherbet down to Cheetah Bee's. We can call an ambulance from there. Quickly!

Foxtrot and Captain carry Sherbet out of room and down corridor.

Captain Be careful now!

Foxtrot Oh, Babe!

Captain Careful.

Captain knocks on Cheetah's door.

Captain Cheetah Bee! Cheetah Bee! Emergency!

Cheetah opens door.

Captain We need an ambulance, Cheetah Bee.

Cheetah Sweet Jesus!

Captain Hurry!

Captain and Foxtrot carry Sherbet into Cheetah's room.

The door is closed behind them.

Very long pause.

Slowly, Cougar stands. He goes to mirror, takes comb from pocket and straightens his hair. When he's satisfied, he searches for his sunglasses and puts them on. He gives himself one last look in the mirror, then strolls round the room. He sees the remains of the birthday cake. He picks up the cake and sits at table. Slowly, he begins to eat cake.

Long pause.

The door opens and Captain enters.

Captain sees Cougar eating cake.

Pause.

Captain closes door behind him, then watches Cougar.

Long pause.

Captain sees gun on floor and picks it up.

Cougar continues to eat.

Pause.

A flashing light illuminates the window. It is the ambulance in the street below.

Captain goes to window.

Captain The ambulance.

Cougar doesn't react.

Pause.

Captain There's Foxtrot. He's crying. Sherbet's on a stretcher. She's crying too.

Pause.

The ambulance drives away.

Captain turns to face Cougar.

Cougar continues to eat cake.

Captain She lost the baby.

Cougar doesn't react.

Pause.

Captain Are you listening, Cougar? She lost the baby.

Cougar doesn't react.

Pause.

Slowly, Captain aims the gun at Cougar.

Cougar is too engrossed in eating the cake to notice.

Pause.

Captain cocks the trigger. It makes a clicking sound.

Still Cougar doesn't look.

Pause.

The door opens and Cheetah appears.

She sees Captain holding gun.

Captain and Cheetah stare at each other, then Captain lowers the gun.

Slowly, Cheetah enters. She takes the gun from Captain and puts it in her coat pocket. She goes back to door, then turns to look back at Captain and Cougar.

Cheetah One day, I went down to the factory to see how the animals were killed. My husband demonstrated on a mink. The animal was spreadeagled on a wooden bench and held in place with straps and chains. Then my husband got a knife and simply started to cut away the skin.

Cougar has stopped eating the cake and is listening.

Cheetah You see, the way to get an immaculate fur is not to kill the animal. The cruelty of it still chills me. But – oh . . .

Feels her fur coat.

It *is* beautiful.

Cheetah exits, closing the door behind her.

Pause.

Captain looks out of window. He opens window and picks up dead bird from window sill.

Captain takes bird over to table and sits opposite Cougar.

Pause.

Captain And the Prince and the Blind Girl lived . . . happily together. And the years flew by them. Years became hours. Hours became seconds. Because The Fastest Clock in the Universe is . . .

Cougar Love.

Captain Hallelujah!

Fade to blackout.

GHOST FROM A PERFECT PLACE

For Tom Yuil –
who knows the shape of truth

What kind of depravity would you not bring about
in order to root out depravity for ever?
Yes, submerge us in filth
and embrace the executioner.
But transform the world.
It needs it!

Bertolt Brecht

Few things are sadder than the truly monstrous.
Nathanael West

The fire is out at the heart of the world;
all tame creatures have grown up wild.
Andrew Motion

Characters

Torchie Sparks
Travis Flood
Rio Sparks
Miss Sulphur
Miss Kerosene

Ghost from a Perfect Place was premièred at the
Hampstead Theatre, London, on 7 April 1994, with
the following cast:

Torchie Sparks Bridget Turner
Travis Flood John Wood
Rio Sparks Trevyn McDowell
Miss Sulphur Rachel Power
Miss Kerosene Katie Tyrrell

Directed by Matthew Lloyd
Designer Laurie Dennett
Lighting Robert Bryan
Artistic Director for Hampstead Theatre Jenny Topper

Act One

A dimly lit room in Bethnal Green, the East End of London. There has been a fire sometime in the past: the walls, floor and woodwork are all badly scorched. A table, two hardbacked chairs, sink, gas oven, armchair – everything bears signs of the blaze. One window reveals a pitch-black night beyond. Two doors: one leading to a bedroom, the other to a wooden landing and stairs leading down to street.

Torchie is sitting on chair. She is sixty-seven years old, but looks much older. She is wearing a black petticoat. Her hair is long and very grey, almost white.

Beside Torchie are a pair of black shoes and a wooden walking-stick. A black dress hangs over back of other chair.

Torchie is just finishing wrapping her left leg in a crepe bandage.

Pause.

A knock on the door.

Torchie glances at door.

Pause.

Another knock.

Torchie Who is it?

    Pause.

    Another knock.

Torchie, her leg now bandaged, picks up walking-stick and limps to door.

Torchie Who is it?

Travis (*off-stage*) Who're you?

Torchie Who am I? I bloody live here. What d'you want?

Travis I'm looking for a girl called Rio.

Torchie That's my granddaughter.

Travis She asked me to meet her here.

Torchie She ain't here yet.

Travis I'll come in and wait, then.

Torchie Lor'struth . . . well, all right, yes. But give me a bloody second. I'm not decent. I'll call when it's safe. Hear me? I'll call when it's safe.

Travis Yes, yes.

Torchie goes back to chair, picks up shoes, then goes into bedroom.

Torchie Safe now!

Travis enters. He is seventy years old and wearing a black, shot-silk, single-breasted suit, white shirt (with gold cuff-links), black tie (with gold tie-pin) and black leather shoes. There is a white silk handkerchief protruding from the top pocket of his jacket and a white lily in his lapel. His very thinning hair is dyed very black. He is holding a bunch of white lilies.

Travis closes door behind him.

He looks at the burnt room.

Torchie (*from bedroom*) You in yet?

Travis . . . Yes.

Pause.

Torchie (*from bedroom*) Lor'struth! I've forgotten my dress! That's your bloody fault, disturbing my routine. Can you see it? Over the back of the chair.

Travis . . . Yes.

Torchie (*from bedroom*) Pass it in to me, will you?

Travis picks up dress and approaches bedroom.

Torchie holds out walking-stick from bedroom.

Torchie (*from bedroom*) No peeking now.

Travis puts dress on walking-stick. Walking-stick and dress disappear back into bedroom.

Travis continues looking at the scorched room.

Pause.

Torchie (*from bedroom*) You been with Rio before?

Travis . . . No.

Torchie (*from bedroom*) When did you meet her?

Travis This afternoon.

Torchie (*from bedroom*) Met her in the graveyard, did you?

Travis Yes.

Torchie (*from bedroom*) She's always there. Her 'patch' she calls it. You go to the graveyard much?

Travis No.

Torchie (*from bedroom*) You can see it from the window. Have a look.

Travis goes to the window and looks out.

Torchie Not exactly the cheeriest of views, is it?

Travis gets a little soot on the cuff of his shirt from the window frame. He tuts irritably and tries – not altogether successfully – to brush it off.

Torchie (*from bedroom*) You lost someone?

Travis What?

Torchie (*from bedroom*) Being in the graveyard.

Travis No, no. I used to live round here. Years ago. I'm back on a visit.

Torchie (*from bedroom*) Seeing how many friends have dropped dead, eh?

Travis Something like that. When I got here, though, I realised I'd forgotten most of them anyway. Everyone just blurs into one nameless face after a while.

Slight pause.

Torchie (*from bedroom*) Easy to forget.

Travis People remember me, though. Oh, yes. Been stopping me all day, they have. Reminding me of the day I shook their hand or called them by their first name. Then they tell me what they've been doing since I've been gone. Very boring.

Torchie (*from bedroom*) What's that?

Travis Other people's stories have never interested me much.

Torchie enters. She is wearing the black dress and the black shoes. She sits at table and starts putting on make-up – pale powder, bright red lipstick, black eyeliner: everything a little too heavy. She barely glances at Travis.

Torchie You'll be gone by the time I get back, I bloody hope.

Slight pause.

Let me give you a word of advice. Do not mess with Rio. One of her men visitors tried to get away without paying a few weeks ago and I found one of his fingernails in the floorboards. So you treat Rio properly. Hear me?

Travis Don't you know who I am?

Torchie gives Travis a quick look then continues with make-up.

Torchie No.

Travis How long have you lived in the East End?

Torchie All my life, for my sins.

Travis Look again.

Torchie looks at Travis.

Pause.

Travis smells the lily in his lapel.

Slowly, a cry of surprise forms at the back of Torchie's throat.

She stands.

Her cry gets louder and louder.

Travis smiles, relishing every moment.

Torchie Travis Flood!

Travis In the flesh.

Torchie Lor'struth! Mr Flood! How can you ever forgive me?

Travis I don't know.

Torchie Mr Travis Flood! You haven't been in these parts since . . .

Travis Nineteen sixty-nine.

Torchie Yes. It must be. That's when they were arresting all the gangsters.

Travis Don't say gangster! I was *not* a gangster! Someone said it to me this afternoon and I lashed out. Broke his nose and robbed him of a few teeth I shouldn't wonder. He won't call me gangster again in a hurry. So . . . no, I was not a gangster. I offered a service. That's all. I was a . . . a businessman.

Torchie Well . . . they were certainly arresting a lot of businessmen in nineteen sixty-nine.

Travis That's why I got away.

Torchie Got away with everything, I'd say.

Travis I didn't mean it like that.

Torchie But you deserved to get away, Mr Flood. The service you offered was a much-needed one. The streets were safe to walk then. Day or night. A lot's changed since then.

Travis Oh, I can see that. Hardly recognised the place. Everything smashed and broken. No order. It's like a wasteland. When I used to be here, you could swim in the canal. Now it's nothing but a sewer. And the graffiti . . . we never used words like that in the heydays. Disgraceful! In the graveyard, I saw some children putting a dead rat in the hands of a stone angel. The kids were filthy too. Pale as ghosts. Zombies. That's what everyone looks like now. Zombies. Where's everyone's self-respect gone? Look at the state of this place. I ask you, what have you all become since I've been gone?

Pause.

Torchie Oh, Mr Flood . . . you . . . you make me feel ashamed. You really do.

Pause.

At least . . . at least I'm wearing my glad-rags and warpaint. Hope that helps de-zombify me a little.

Travis A little.

Torchie You look a vision, though, Mr Flood. Can I say that? You look just as much a . . . a king – yes! A king! – as you did in the . . . in the heydays, to use your word. You look a million dollars.

Travis Don't undersell me. That's practically the price of this suit alone.

Torchie Silk is it, Mr Flood?

Travis Shot silk, yes.

Torchie I adore the feel of silk.

Travis holds out arm.

Travis Have a stroke.

Torchie Oh, I don't like to, Mr Flood.

Travis *I'd* like you to.

Gingerly, Torchie steps forward and touches Travis's sleeve.

Torchie Oh, it's divine, Mr Flood. That's the only word for it. You know what you've got, Mr Flood? Pizzazz! Pizzazz by the bucketload and no mistake. They broke the mould when they made you. The mould marked pizzazz was smashed for ever.

Pause.

Mr Flood . . . do you remember me?

Slight pause.

Travis No.

Torchie We used to speak, Mr Flood.

Travis I spoke to lots of people.

Torchie I had long black hair in those days. And a beautiful figure, so I was told.

Travis Well, your hair's still long at any rate.

Torchie Let me give you a clue, Mr Flood. Every Saturday night!

Travis Every Saturday night?

Torchie That's when you and your boys would visit us. Me and my husband. Ring any bells?

Travis Not a tinkle. What's your name?

Torchie You'll twig it soon, Mr Flood. I'm sure you will!

Travis I doubt it.

Torchie Well, if you don't, you don't.

Slight pause.

You know what you being here has made me feel, Mr Flood?

Travis Ain't got a clue.

Torchie Chosen. It's true! Now I know how Moses must have felt when he saw the burning bush. He must have looked at those flames and heard it jabbering away nineteen to the dozen, and he must have thought, Lor'struth! Why me?

Pause.

Travis holds lilies out to Torchie.

Travis You might as well have these?

Torchie But they were for Rio surely?

Travis You'll probably appreciate them more.

Torchie You always understood people so well, Mr Flood.

Travis It's nothing.

Torchie It's everything! If you don't mind me saying so. Gestures like this. Flowers from the heydays . . .

Slowly, Torchie steps forward and takes flowers from Travis.

She holds them as if they're priceless.

Travis starts idly brushing at the soot on his cuff again.

Torchie Mr Flood – your cuff!

Travis What?

Torchie Your sleeve! That's not soot, is it?

Travis Yes. From the window frame.

Torchie That's my fault. Telling you to look at the graveyard and not warning you of the soot. I could hang myself. I'll get a cloth.

Torchie puts flowers on table, then goes to sink.

She starts damping a flannel.

Travis Don't trouble yourself.

Torchie Ain't no trouble at all, Mr Flood. Here's you giving me flowers, and how do I repay you? I soil your beautiful clothes.

Torchie returns to Travis with flannel.

Torchie indicates a chair.

Torchie Please. Sit down, Mr Flood.

Travis takes step towards chair, then hesitates.

Torchie Don't worry. The chairs have been thoroughly de-sooted.

Travis sits.

Torchie tries to kneel beside him, but it's obviously both difficult and painful with her damaged leg.

Travis Here! You sit. I'll stand.

Stands.

Torchie I wouldn't hear of it, Mr Flood.

Travis But it's hurting you.

Torchie What I deserve. My punishment. Now . . . just got to get the drumstick in place.

Torchie continues to settle herself. She yells out in pain a few times.

Travis watches, getting increasingly agitated.

With one last cry Torchie gets her leg settled.

Torchie There!

Slowly, Travis sits again.

Torchie is dabbing at Travis's cuff.

Travis looks round at room.

Torchie There was a terrible fire, Mr Flood..

Travis I can see that.

Torchie Almost a year ago now.

Slight pause.

One night . . . one night I woke up and . . . What are those flies called, Mr Flood? Flies that look like they're on fire.

Travis . . . Fireflies?

Slight pause.

Torchie One night I woke up and the air was full of fireflies. Lor'struth they were beautiful. Then one of the fireflies landed on my blanket. It turned into a flame. And I just lay there, Mr Flood. In a burning bed. Watching. The wallpaper caught fire. It turned to ash and floated in the air. That does look pretty, I thought. My face was tingling in the heat. Eyes were watering. But did I move? No. I just lay there. Calmly watching the whole world burn up around me. And d'you know something, Mr Flood? It was the most peaceful I'd ever been.

Pause.

Lucky to get out alive, I was.

Travis But you did, obviously.

Torchie Only because of Rio. She'd been woken by the fireflies as well. Only she had the sense to know what they were. Lor'struth, I might not be the sharpest knife in the dishwater, but even I should have twigged you don't get many fireflies in Bethnal Green.

Travis You got out safe and sound. That's the main thing.

Torchie Safe, yes. But not altogether sound, Mr Flood.

Touches her bandaged leg.

Travis Ah, I see.

Torchie My dancing days were over anyway.

Travis Must have been very painful.

Torchie There were times I screamed 'Cut it off! I'd rather hop around than go through this!' A terrible time. But you know who helped me through it all, don't you?

Travis Who?

Torchie Rio, of course.

Travis Of course.

Torchie She looks after me, Mr Flood. She's the bread-winner.

Travis I'm well aware of that.

Torchie We have to live! If it wasn't for Rio, we'd be on the streets. Oh, I know what some people think. And I know it would never have happened in the heydays. Believe me, I never thought I'd end up living like this. But sometimes you have no choice. I love Baby Rio and Baby Rio loves me. She might be a little rough and ready on the outside, but inside she's got a heart of gold.

  Slight pause.

Travis I'm sure she has. A heart of pure gold. Just like her grandmother.

Torchie Thank you, Mr Flood.

Travis And her mother, I have no doubt.

Torchie Oh . . .

  Slight pause.

Travis What?

  Torchie begins to get up.

Once more, it causes her pain.

Travis goes to help.

Torchie Don't help.

Finally, Torchie gets to her feet.

She takes flannel back to sink.

Torchie You touched a heartache just then, Mr Flood. A great heartache.

Slight pause.

Travis Your daughter?

Torchie My Donna, yes. My beautiful Donna. Rio's mother. Do you remember her?

Travis No.

Torchie She adored you when she was a child, Mr Flood.

Travis I have a way with children.

Torchie I'll say you did, Mr Flood. Me and Donna were down Bethnal Green Road market one day. She must have been . . . oh, six at the time. And, Lor'struth, she was bawling her eyes out. You know the way children get. Crying for no reason other than the need to make tears. I bought her some popcorn. She loved popcorn, my Donna. Always smelt of it.

Travis Popcorn was her perfume.

Torchie You remember!

Travis . . . No.

Pause.

Torchie You appeared, Mr Flood. Just as much a vision then as you are now. And you saw my crying Donna and

you looked so sad. You took the white lily from your
lapel and you gave it to her. Instantly, her crying stopped.
Then you got in your car and drove away, as if it was
the most natural thing in the world for you to end
the heartache of children. Oh, I treasured that flower,
Mr Flood. Like it was a splinter from the Cross itself.

Pause.

Travis I gave my lilies to lots of people.

Torchie You did?

Torchie sits opposite Travis.

Travis glances at his wristwatch.

Pause.

Torchie Well, perhaps it's best that you can't remember
Donna. You'd be so upset if you knew what happened to
her.

Pause.

It was terrible.

Pause.

I see a bruise.

Travis A bruise?

Torchie A bruise on my Donna. But it ain't a normal
sort of bruise. Lor'struth, no. If I tell you where it was,
Mr Flood, perhaps you can guess what kind of bruise it
is.

Touches her neck.

It's here!

Slight pause.

Travis . . . A lovebite?

Torchie A lovebite it is, Mr Flood.

Travis How old is she?

Torchie Well, she's no longer the six-year-old girl you gave the lily to, Mr Flood. That was in the beginning of the heydays. No, we're at the end of the heydays now. Nineteen sixty-nine. And, although my Donna might still have her hair in a pony-tail and smell of popcorn, she's fourteen years old. And she's standing in front of me – in this very room – with a lovebite on her neck. She's trying to hide it under her blouse collar . . . but there it is! 'Who did that, Donna?' I ask. She don't want to tell me. 'Is it someone at school . . .? All right, all right! Don't get in a mood. Just make sure your dad doesn't see it. He'll hit the roof if he does and kill the boy to boot. And I hope you ain't doing anything silly – Where are you going? Don't storm into the bedroom! I ain't finished with you yet, young lady!' But I don't pry any more, Mr Flood. I've got to allow her some privacy, haven't I? It's only a lovebite. No harm in it. I won't ask any more questions. It's the right thing to do, don't you think, Mr Flood? Tell me it's the right thing to do!

Travis Yes, it's right.

Torchie Wrong!

Slight pause.

It's a few months later now, Mr Flood. I'm waiting for my Donna to come home from school. Quarter past four. She should be here any minute. I start making tea. Half past four. She's probably chatting with a friend. She's very sociable. Five o'clock.

Starts pacing the room.

She's never been this late before, Mr Flood. Not without telling me. Lor'struth, she knows how I worry. I'm imagining all sorts of things.

Goes to window.

There's no sign of her, Mr Flood! 'Donna! Donna!' Half past five. I know something's wrong, Mr Flood. What shall I do? If I go out to look for her, she might come back while I'm out. Or, if there has been an accident, the police might come. I'm a nervous wreck . . . And then the door opens. 'Where have you bloody been, you naughty girl! It's nearly six o'clock. I'm out of my mind with worry . . . What's wrong? . . . You went to see the doctor? But, why, Donna? What's wrong with you . . .?' And what does she tell me, Mr Flood? What words come out of her mouth?

Travis She's pregnant!

Torchie I should have asked more questions when I saw the lovebite. 'Donna, you've got to tell me who the boy is . . . He's responsible. He's got to pay.' She won't tell me, Mr Flood. Not a word. She's crying. I stroke her hair. And all I'm thinking is, How am I going to tell Mr Sparks?

Travis Mr Sparks?

Torchie My husband. He's a religious man, Mr Flood. He can quote the Bible and often does. And . . . oh, he adores little Donna. She's his little princess. He's standing there, Mr Flood. By the window. 'Now calm yourself!' He starts trembling. 'We've got to help our Donna!' He's going very red. 'No! Leave her alone!' He's hitting Donna, Mr Flood. 'Stop it! Stop it! She won't tell you the boy's name! I've asked her a million times! Stop!' He's beating her black and blue! Her nose is bleeding. Stop him, Mr Flood! Stop him! Stop him!

Travis Stop!

Slight pause.

Has he stopped?

Torchie Yes, Mr Flood. It's later now. We're discussing what to do. We ain't got any idea. Our little girl pregnant. The father unknown. Oh, what can we do?

Travis Abortion.

Torchie We could never have allowed that, Mr Flood. Not in the heydays. We've just got to go through with it. Donna will have the child. We won't press to find out who the boy is. Mr Sparks will pray to God to forgive his sinning daughter. And everything will work out all right in the end! Right, Mr Flood?

Travis Right!

Torchie Wrong!

Slight pause.

Lor'struth!

Travis What is it?

Torchie Can't you hear it?

Travis What?

Torchie Screaming! Coming from in there!

She indicates bedroom.

There it is again!

Travis It's Donna?

Torchie She's having the baby, Mr Flood. Sooner than we thought.

Approaches bedroom.

'Shush, Donna! Don't worry! Mummy's here!'

Looks into bedroom.

Oh, she's bleeding! Blood everywhere. What shall I do, Mr Flood?

Travis Where's your husband?

Torchie He ain't here!

Travis Get a doctor!

Torchie And leave Donna alone! Another scream! I'm going to panic, Mr Flood.

Travis Don't!

Torchie Then bloody tell me what to do?

Travis . . . Boil some water!

Torchie Good idea. But it does no good.

Travis What d'you mean?

Torchie The screams, Mr Flood. Can't you hear them? They're getting louder and louder.

Rushes into bedroom.

Pause.

Travis Wh . . . what's happening?

Torchie A baby girl, Mr Flood. My Donna's given birth to a beautiful baby – Ahhhh!

Travis What is it?

Torchie She's dead, Mr Flood!

Travis What? The baby?

Torchie Lor'struth! Not the baby!

Enters.

How can it be the bloody baby? She grew up to meet you in the graveyard this afternoon. Now pay attention!

Goes back into bedroom.

Slight pause.

Travis It's your daughter.

Torchie enters, looking stricken.

Torchie My Donna was too good for this place, Mr Flood.

Travis She was.

Torchie The good die young.

Travis They do.

Torchie and Travis sit.

Pause.

Torchie I called the baby Rio. Donna always liked Westerns, you see.

Travis Very good.

Torchie And I've brought up Baby Rio all by myself. She reminds me of Donna in so many ways. The way she smiles. Or threads her fingers together.

Pause.

You ever have any children, Mr Flood?

Travis No. But I can imagine that losing –

Torchie No, you can't. Only a parent can imagine what losing a child must be like. You see, your child is everything, Mr Flood. It's your future. When I lost my daughter . . .

Travis Don't think about it. It's over.

Torchie I've spent a lifetime thinking about it. It will never be over.

Slight pause.

Travis You'll make me cry if you cry.

Torchie Lor'struth, Mr Flood. I've done all my crying. No tears left. I'm as dry as a desert where that's concerned. Besides, you ain't come back after all these years to hear my heartache.

Travis If it helps you to burden me, I don't mind.

Torchie *I* mind.

Sight pause.

Shall I tell you something funny?

Travis That'd be a relief.

Torchie Look around.

Travis What?

Torchie Just look. Go on.

Travis looks round.

Torchie Now if you can remember my name, you'll have a bit of a chuckle.

Travis Your name's Sparks.

Torchie You remember!

Travis No.

Torchie Then how – ?

Travis You told me your husband's name was Mr Sparks.

Slight pause.

But – yes – it *is* funny. The Sparks family living in a burnt house. Very droll.

Torchie I've got a sense of humour ain't I, Mr Flood?

Travis No one has the ability to laugh at their misfortunes like the women of the East End.

Torchie And I bet you've met lots of women, Mr Flood.

Travis Some of the most glamorous in the world. But they bore me. You know why? No humour. Something goes wrong – a car crash or some minor disfigurement – and it's nothing but long faces and feeling sorry for themselves. But you! Not a bit of it. Your whole world falls to pieces and you still crack a joke. I tell you, I'd rather look at your legs and hear your sense of humour, than look at their million-dollar legs and listen to their humourless drivel any day. It's a privilege to have your humour to entertain me. And that's no exaggeration, Mrs Sparks.

Torchie Oh, you never called me Mrs Sparks.

Travis I didn't?

Torchie Lor'struth, no.

Travis What did I call you then?

Torchie By my nickname. Like everyone else. You'd call it out every Saturday night. Remember?

Travis No.

Torchie You will.

Travis I won't.

Torchie You might.

Travis Just bloody tell me. We ain't got all night.

Torchie True. But we've got until my granddaughter turns up.

Pause.

Travis I want to show you something.

Travis takes a paperback book from his pocket.

Torchie A book.

She peers closer.

With your name on it!

She peers closer still.

The Man with the White Lily. Lor'struth, Mr Flood. That's you! You were the man with the white lily.

Travis I've written the story of my life. It's why I've come back. To do some publicity. See the photograph on the back?

Travis shows Torchie back cover of book.

Torchie Oh . . . Mr Flood! A heyday you! In your black suit and tie. And the lily, of course. Pure pizzazz.

Travis offers book out to her.

Travis Have a good look. Go on.

Torchie hesitates a moment, then wipes her hands on her dress and takes the book almost reverentially.

She sighs and stares at photograph for a moment.

Torchie All the girls used to swoon over you, Mr Flood. You were their flame.

Travis I know.

Torchie opens book.

Torchie 'Chapter One . . . Once, long ago, I was born in a paradise called Bethnal Green –' Oh, that's beautiful, Mr Flood. Really. You make it sound like a fairy-tale. But you're right! That's exactly what the heydays seem like.

Flicks through the pages.

Oh, look! The heyday church!

Flicks page.

And the heyday pub!

Flicks page.

The heyday market! Where I used to shop. Where you gave Donna that lily. Used to get my cheese and ham there. And there . . . there's the butcher's. I was in there one day when you walked in, Mr Flood. You didn't see me. Why should you? The shop was full. And, of course, there was no queuing for you. 'Here comes Mr Flood,' people said. And we parted like the Red Sea. You were with two of your boys. They had black suits on. Just like you. There you stood. In the middle of the butcher's, looking at all the meat. Then you pointed at half a cow hanging from a meathook. Sawn clean in half it was. Its insides showing and everything. You snapped your fingers and your two boys took the carcass down. Blood was still dripping everywhere. Your boys carried it out of the butcher's and threw it in the back of your car. There was blood all over their suits. And across the pavement. But not a drop on you.

Slight pause.

Travis What a memory you have.

Torchie Any second of the heydays is more real to me than anything that's happened since. When I think of the heydays it's like thinking of . . . of another place. Does that sound foolish? I suppose it does. But I can't help it. The heydays are like a perfect place for me. A perfect place I visited once, but can never visit again.

Long pause.

Goes to give book back to Travis.

Travis Keep it.

Torchie Keep it?

Travis A gift.

Torchie Lor'struth, Mr Flood. Where will your generosity end?

Clutches book to her chest.

Will you do something for me, Mr Flood?

Travis If I can.

Torchie Will you sign it for me?

Travis Delighted.

Takes book.

Slight pause.

Knowing your name might help.

Torchie Every Saturday night you'd visit. Every Saturday night you'd see me. And every Saturday night you'd call, 'Evening, Torchie!'

Travis Torchie! That's your nickname?

Torchie nods.

Travis Well, I'm glad we've got that over and done with.

246

Torchie You still don't remember me though, do you, Mr Flood?

Travis Not a thing.

Signs book.

'To Torchie. Warmest wishes, Travis Flood.'

Hands book back to Torchie.

Torchie I'll worship it. This and the lilies – The lilies! Lors'truth! I best put them in some water.

Puts book on table, then gets vase from cupboard and fills it with water.

I've got some serious arranging to do. I used to love flowers in the heydays.

Takes vase over to table and spreads flowers out.

Mr Sparks used to buy me flowers for my birthday.

Travis How long has he been dead?

Torchie Who?

Travis Your husband.

Torchie Mr Sparks ain't dead, Mr Flood.

Travis But you said . . . I'm *sure* you said you brought your granddaughter up all by yourself.

Torchie I did.

Goes to drawer and removes a pair of extremely large silver scissors.

Holds scissors in the air, snipping them.

Scissors!

Goes back to flowers and starts trimming the stalks.

Pause.

Oh, no, Mr Sparks is not dead.

Continues snipping stalks.

Slight pause.

Travis He left you, then?

Torchie No. Mr Sparks didn't leave me.

Travis So what happened?

Torchie Oh, you don't want to keep hearing my heartache.

Travis I do.

Pause.

Torchie Praying!

Travis Praying?

Torchie That's what I can hear, Mr Flood. Mr Sparks praying. He ain't bloody stopped since the day Donna was buried. I try to help him, but what can I do? I have a baby to look after. I ain't got no time to grieve. But for Mr Sparks, grief is all he has. I've heard of the phrase 'mad with grief' but I've never seen it until now. It breaks your heart to see him.

Travis Where is he?

Torchie Sitting over there. By the window. See him? Staring at the night sky. See him?

Travis . . . Yes.

Torchie And he's praying, Mr Flood. Endless whispered prayers.

Travis I hear him.

Torchie 'You've got to pull yourself together. Baby Rio needs us. Donna is dead. There's nothing we can do about that! And – Lor'struth – your praying is giving me a headache!' He's mumbling something now. 'What's that? . . . A comet? . . . Where?'

Goes to window and looks out.

'No. I can't see a comet!' But he can, Mr Flood. He can see it blazing over Bethnal Green. And, suddenly, he's up, Mr Flood! He's rushing out! He's rushing to the roof. I want to run after him. But Baby Rio is crying! She's screaming! What shall I do, Mr Flood? Run after Mr Sparks or comfort Baby Rio? Baby Rio might be choking! What shall I do, Mr Flood? Tell me! Tell me!

Travis Comfort the baby!

Torchie Thank you, Mr Flood. Here I am! Rocking her in my arms. 'Shush now, Baby Rio.' She stops crying. There! It was the right decision, wasn't it, Mr Flood? To comfort Baby Rio and not run after Mr Sparks? Right?

Travis Right!

Torchie Wrong! Because it's while I'm rocking Baby Rio I hear the crash. Something has fallen from the roof, Mr Flood. Will you look out of the window and tell me what you can see, please?

Travis hesitates.

Torchie I can't go! I've got the baby in my arms.

Slowly, Travis gets up.

He goes to window and – being careful of the soot – looks out.

Travis It's Mr Sparks?

Torchie Yes, Mr Flood. He tried to kill himself.

Travis But he's not dead?

Torchie No.

Travis Injured?

Torchie It was his brain, Mr Flood. The hospital did what they could. But . . . but he's like a child now, Mr Flood. Stares at me with wide, empty eyes. And he just mumbles and gurgles. He ain't said a word I've understood in twenty-five years.

Travis He's been in hospital for twenty-five years!

Torchie I visit him every night. Where I was going when you turned up.

Slight pause.

Travis That last year of the heydays everything changed. It was a bad year for me.

Torchie For you! What about *me*, Mr Flood! Imagine what it was like for *me*! At the beginning of the year I was happy. I had a husband. A daughter. All I ever wanted. By the end of the year my daughter was dead. My husband little more than a vegetable. And a baby granddaughter to bring up single-handed. Oh, yes, for me the heydays were well and truly over.

Long pause.

Did I do something, Mr Flood? Was I being punished for some sin? Was I cursed, Mr Flood? Cursed!

Travis I try not to think like that.

Torchie It's hard not to sometimes.

Pause.

Travis Torchie?

Torchie Mr Flood?

Travis Why don't you put the kettle on? I'm gasping for a cup of tea.

Torchie Of course, Mr Flood. Lor'struth, I should have offered you one earlier. Whatever will you think of me?

Puts kettle on.

Starts getting cups, milk, sugar, tea-bags, etc.

Travis It's been years since I've had a traditional East End cuppa.

Torchie Well, we'll soon put that right.

Slight pause.

Travis I tell you what, Torchie. I could just murder some bickies if you've got any.

Torchie I should have.

Torchie gets packet of biscuits.

She finds it almost empty.

Torchie Oh, look at this! Rio and her bloody mates've been at them. They're like a plague of locusts, those girls. Only two left. I hope that's enough for you, Mr Flood.

Torchie puts both biscuits by Travis.

Travis (*giving Torchie back a biscuit*) We'll have one each, Torchie.

Torchie (*giving Travis back the biscuit*) You asked for them.

Travis (*giving Torchie the biscuit*) One is fine.

Torchie (*giving Travis the biscuit*) But you're hungry.

Travis (*giving Torchie the biscuit*) Not that hungry.

Torchie (*giving Travis the biscuit*) It's only fair.

Travis (*giving Torchie the biscuit*) It's not fair at all.

Torchie (*giving Travis the biscuit*) You're the guest, Mr Flood.

Travis (*angrily, giving Torchie the biscuit*) Just have a bloody bicky!

> *Torchie tenses and stares at Travis.*
>
> *Long pause.*
>
> *The kettle boils.*
>
> *Torchie finishes making tea and gives Travis a cup.*
>
> *Then she sits at table with her cup.*
>
> *They both dunk biscuits in the tea.*
>
> *Very long pause.*

Travis Can I ask you something, Torchie?

Torchie What?

Travis Have I aged much?

Torchie Well, your hair's the same colour at any rate.

Travis I watch my waistline.

Torchie Good for you.

> *Slight pause.*

Travis Twenty lengths a day.

Torchie Twenty lengths?

Travis Of my swimming-pool.

Torchie *Your* swimming-pool?

Travis *My* swimming-pool in *my* garden. Designed the whole thing myself, I did.

Torchie Oh . . . Mr Flood!

Travis 'It'll cost a fortune,' they said. 'We'll have to uproot those palm trees and dig up that cactus.' 'Well, you better start uprooting and digging, then, hadn't you,' I told them. 'Because I want to be floating on a lilo and sipping pina colada by the end of the month.'

Torchie I had a pina colada once.

Travis You strike me as a pina colada sort of woman.

Torchie That's one of the nicest things anyone's ever said to me.

Travis Then your life's been short of nice things.

Torchie It has, Mr Flood. Did they finish your pool in time?

Travis Naturally. They knew I meant business. I ain't a man to mess with when my mind's set on something, as well you know, Torchie. Now I float and sip in the most beautiful pool in all Hollywood.

Torchie Hollywood?

Travis Where I live now.

Torchie Must be heaven.

Travis Near as damn. I'll tell you my typical day, shall I? A day in heaven with Travis Flood. I wake up. What do I feel? Silk sheets. What do I see? Golden sunlight coming through the windows. I get up, then take my breakfast out to the poolside –

Torchie You don't make your own breakfast, surely?

Travis No . . . My butler does that. Then I have a swim. Sip those pina coladas you like to get drunk on, Torchie. Then I get dressed and cruise about in my black Cadillac.

Torchie You always liked black cars.

Travis Where shall we go today? The mountains? The beach?

Torchie Beach! If it ain't too far.

Travis mimes driving car.

Travis No distance in this car. Best suspension in the world.

Torchie Hardly know you're moving.

Travis Notice the palm trees. And yellow sand far as the eye can see.

Torchie Can we sunbathe?

Travis That's dangerous, Torchie. Sun-rays give you cancer.

Torchie Daylight didn't harm us in the heydays, did it, Mr Flood?

Travis Put this sunblock on and we'll go shark fishing in my boat.

Torchie Shark fishing!

Travis I'll put some bait on the fishing-hook.

Travis mimes putting bait on hook.

Torchie What d'you use, Mr Flood?

Travis Steak.

Torchie Steak! I'd never have thought sharks had a taste for steak. Not many cows in the ocean, after all, are there?

Travis Anything bloody will do.

Pause.

Travis Not boring you, Torchie?

Torchie Ain't had such a good time in years.

Slight pause.

Travis I've got something! Good God, it's a big one! There! Torchie! You see it?

Torchie Where?

Travis There! The shark! Jumping in and out of the ocean.

Torchie It's huge! Don't let it get away!

Travis I won't! Come here, you devil!

Torchie Pull, Mr Flood!

Travis It's coming! Look at the jaws!

Torchie So many teeth.

Travis There! On the deck. Be careful, Torchie. It's still alive.

Torchie What a monster!

Travis Watch it die!

Torchie and Travis watch the imaginary shark in front of them.

Torchie is becoming worried and uncomfortable.

Travis What's wrong, Torchie?

Torchie It's suffering, Mr Flood.

Travis Not for much longer.

Torchie But its fin's all a-quiver. It's in pain . . . Oh the poor thing . . . Chuck it back, Mr Flood!

Travis What about dinner? You can have shark steaks!

Torchie I'd rather have a rissole! Please, Mr Flood! Before it's too late.

Torchie is becoming increasingly agitated.

Travis All right, all right.

Travis kicks imaginary shark back into the ocean.

Travis There! Off it goes.

Torchie I . . . I want to go home now.

Travis Yes, go home.

Torchie Let's sit by the swimming-pool.

Travis We'll watch the sunset.

Torchie Then go to bed.

Travis What d'you feel?

Torchie Silk sheets.

Slight pause.

Travis And that, Torchie, is my day in heaven.

Pause.

Torchie Life's been good to you, Mr Flood.

Travis It has.

Torchie Someone up there likes you.

Travis They must.

Torchie All happy ever after for you.

Pause.

Travis Yes.

Pause.

Torchie To think . . . you're one of our own made good. You don't mind me saying that, do you?

Travis I'm proud of it. When people ask me where I'm from I don't say 'England' or 'London', I say, 'I'm a Bethnal Green lad born and bred.' Ain't lost my accent, have I?

Torchie Not at all.

Travis I practise it. Every day.

Slight pause.

Can I tell you something, Torchie? I might have everything a heart desires, but sometimes . . . sometimes I'm lonely. Lonely for this place. And salt-of-the-earth people like yourself.

Lifts cup.

To the heydays.

Torchie To the heydays.

Travis and Torchie clink cups and drink some tea.

Pause.

Travis reaches out and gives Torchie's hand a squeeze.

Torchie is visibly moved.

Pause.

Torchie Mr Flood, I'd like to show you something.

Travis What, Torchie?

Torchie I don't usually show anyone. But tonight . . . this special night . . . for you . . . Mr Flood, will you look the other way? And don't look round till I tell you? Will you do that for me please?

Travis looks the other way.

Torchie goes into bedroom.

Travis Mind if I smoke, Torchie?

Torchie (*from bedroom*) It's hardly likely to bother me after my house nearly burnt down, is it now, Mr Flood?

Travis You have a remarkable way of looking at things, Torchie.

Travis takes a large cigar and box of matches from his pocket.

He lights cigar with match.

Torchie reappears.

She has an old-fashioned cinema serving-tray around her neck and is holding a torch: cinema usherette items from the 1960s.

She goes to the main light switch and turns light off.

Torchie You can look now, Mr Flood.

Travis turns.

Torchie lights up her serving-tray.

It is very bright.

Torchie Can I see your ticket please?

Travis (*laughing*) Well, look at this. Look at you, Torchie. Torchie! Of course! Torchie!

Torchie Smoking or non-smoking, sir?

Travis (*laughing*) Oh . . . er . . . smoking, I guess.

Torchie This way, sir.

Travis stands.

Torchie switches her torch on.

It shines directly into Travis's eyes.

It dazzles him.

Travis Lor'struth, Torchie.

Travis rubs his eyes.

Torchie is walking round the room, as if showing someone to their seat in the cinema.

Torchie Cigarettes! Ice cream! Programmes!

Travis suddenly stops laughing.

He is looking troubled now.

He stares at Torchie.

Torchie notices Travis's expression.

Torchie What is it, Mr Flood?

Travis continues to stare.

Torchie Lor'struth, you look like you're going to faint. You better sit down.

Torchie helps Travis to his seat.

Travis . . . I remember!

Torchie You remember!

Travis . . . Everything!

Torchie Me and my husband.

Travis The local cinema! You ran it!

Torchie The Empress, yes. And you remember my little Donna?

Travis Donna! The girl from the cinema! Oh, my God. It was *her*!

Torchie I know, Mr Flood. It gets me that way sometimes – And look! Here!

She takes a pressed flower from the tray.

It's the lily you gave my Donna. All those years ago. Pressed flat as paper. Still with us.

Torchie holds flower out to Travis.

He stares at it, horrified.

Torchie sits and watches Travis.

Pause.

Torchie Those days mean as much to you as they do to me, don't they, Mr Flood? I ran back into the flames to save these few things. But – Lor'struth – they were worth getting a drumstick for. You understand that, don't you, Mr Flood?

Pause.

Travis Torchie . . .

Torchie Yes, Mr Flood?

Travis I did . . . things. During the heydays. Things I'd . . . forgotten.

Torchie I forget some things too –

Travis No, no. That's not what I meant! The things I did . . . I . . . I forget them because . . . I had to forget.

Torchie Had to?

Travis I *made* myself forget.

Torchie I'm . . . not sure I understand you, Mr Flood.

Slight pause.

Travis Torchie . . . seeing you like this. How it all went wrong for you. From that one . . . terrible thing. What happened to your daughter . . .

Torchie Oh, I understand you now, Mr Flood.

Travis No, no, you can't.

Torchie But I do. You're trying to say you should have stopped it in some way.

Travis Stopped it?

Torchie You were there to protect us.

Travis . . . Well, yes, but . . .

Torchie So you should have prevented what happened.

Travis Oh, yes.

Torchie But you mustn't think that way, Mr Flood.

Travis I mustn't?

Torchie No. You see, this is what I believe. We don't get away with anything in this life. Everything has to be paid for. So, whoever was responsible for . . . what happened to my Donna, well, he'll get his punishment. And I hope he shrieks in agony for all the suffering he's caused.

  Pause.

Travis So much lost, Torchie.

  Pause.

Torchie We don't lose anything, Mr Flood. Not really. One day I was sitting here when I felt a chill. I came out in goose-bumps. Goose-bumps so big you could hang your hat on them. Someone's just walked over my grave, I thought. And then . . . then I could smell her. Like burying my head in her clothes. Popcorn! And I knew, Mr Flood. Knew my Donna was in the room with me.

Travis stares at Torchie.

Pause.

Torchie Everything was very quiet, Mr Flood . . . And then . . . then I saw something . . . Hazy mist. And the mist took shape. Arms, legs, a white dress . . . It was the ghost of my Donna, Mr Flood.

Pause.

She spoke to me.

Travis What did she say?

Torchie That she was happy.

Travis Nothing else?

Torchie That's all I needed.

Slight pause.

From that day on, Mr Flood, I've been able to call her to me. I just say her name. And . . . oh, if I say it with every bit of love in my heart, she comes back. Like a daughter should. Let me call her now, Mr Flood. So you can have a word with her.

Travis I . . . well, I don't believe in ghosts so –

Torchie Donna!

Travis Don't!

Torchie Too late! Can't you feel? The chill?

Pause.

Travis . . . Yes.

Torchie Goose-bumps! And you too, Mr Flood. I can see them.

Travis Can't you stop her?

Torchie Someone's just walked over my grave.

Sniffs.

Popcorn!

Travis gets to his feet.

Travis Oh, stop her.

Torchie Donna! Mr Flood has returned to visit us. And look . . . Here's the lily he gave you.

Holds the pressed lily out.

She's almost here, Mr Flood.

Very still and silent.

Long pause.

Then . . . the front door – which is behind Torchie and Travis – swings silently open.

Rio stands in doorway.

Rio is twenty-five years old. Her hair is blonde and tied in a pony-tail. She is very pale and thin, sickly almost, yet still – despite all the odds – hauntingly beautiful. She is wearing a tacky gold-sequinned mini-skirt, a shiny, gold T-shirt, a threadbare denim jacket (decorated with gold sequins and rhinestones) and boots (spray-painted gold).

Slight pause.

Rio turns main lights on and enters.

Travis and Torchie are startled.

Torchie Lor'struth, Baby Rio! You nearly scared me to bloody death! My heart's going to explode, I swear it is – Now don't look at me like that. I know I should have gone by now. But Mr Flood arrived a little early and . . .

well, we've been having a good old natter. Reminiscing about the heydays. Ain't we, Mr Flood?

Rio has flopped in armchair.

Travis is staring at Rio.

Slight pause.

Torchie So many memories come back, Baby Rio . . . Mr Flood used to visit us. Every Saturday night it was. 'Evening, Torchie,' he'd call. Mr Flood remembers everything as if it was yesterday. Just like I do – Oh, all right, all right, Baby Rio. I'm going. You see the way she's looking at me, Mr Flood.

Torchie starts to put coat on, etc.

Travis continues staring at Rio.

Slight pause.

Torchie Mr Flood's written a book, Baby Rio. You see it there? *The Man with the White Lily*. There's a heyday photo of him on the back. Pure pizzazz. And there's more photos inside. The heyday church. The heyday pub. The heyday market – All right, all right. I'm nearly ready.

Torchie picks up walking-stick.

Travis continues staring at Rio.

Slight pause.

Torchie He brought flowers, Baby Rio. You see? That proves what a gentleman he is. A gentleman from the heydays – All right, all right, stop giving me that look.

Slight pause.

He lives in Hollywood now, Baby Rio. Got his own swimming pool. Butler. Black Cadillac. Speedboat.

He goes fishing. Guess what for, Baby Rio . . . Sharks!
Can you believe that? And you'd never guess what
sharks eat – All right, all right, I'm off.

Slight pause.

Stay till I get back if you like, Mr Flood. I don't mind at
all. I'll cook some tea. A traditional East End something
or other. Whatever you like – All right, all right . . . She's
got a heart of gold really, Mr Flood.

Torchie exits.

Long pause.

Rio What d'you want, Travis?

Slight pause.

I'll do anything.

Slight pause.

I don't care.

Pause.

Travis I want you to . . . tell me.

Rio Tell you what?

Travis Things. About yourself.

Rio Sex things?

Travis No. Things about . . . your life.

Rio gets up and approaches Travis.

Travis backs away.

Travis What're you doing?

Rio makes advances towards Travis.

Travis No! Don't!

Rio gropes Travis.

Travis Don't!

Rio stops.

Pause.

Rio Money.

Travis . . . What?

Rio Pay me.

Travis But I don't want . . . any of that. I want you to talk.

Rio I don't talk!

Slight pause.

Travis Then I don't pay.

Slight pause.

Rio glances towards window.

Travis follows her glance.

Travis Oh . . . I get it! Of course! The rest of your gang are waiting for you. In the graveyard. I suppose one call from you and they'll be over here like the zombies they are.

Rio stares.

Travis And . . . I suppose I'll end up like the others who messed with you. Fingernails in the floorboards . . . Oh, yes, your grandmother warned me . . . I know what you're thinking. Why's he doing this? So little money. Why make a fuss . . . ?

Pause.

Because I'm Travis Flood. That's why.

Pause.

Travis makes for the door.

Rio steps towards him.

Rio Don't, Travis.

Pause.

Travis hesitates.

Rio takes step towards him.

Pause.

Suddenly, Travis makes up his mind.

He rushes for door.

Rio dashes to him and savagely kicks him.

Travis staggers back into room, falls to his knees.

Travis I'm . . . Travis Flood!

Rio kicks and hits him.

Travis collapses.

Pause.

Rio goes over to window and –

Rio *(calling)* Girls!

Blackout.

Act Two

Travis is tied to a chair with various things, mainly tights.

Rio, Miss Sulphur and Miss Kerosene are sitting round table.

Miss Sulphur is eighteen; Miss Kerosene is twelve. Like Rio, they have their hair in pony-tails and are wearing gold-sequinned mini-skirts, etc. Also, like Rio, they are possessed of a languid barbarity.

Collectively, Rio, Miss Sulphur and Miss Kerosene are known as the Cheerleaders.

Miss Sulphur is preparing to put make-up on Miss Kerosene's face. Rio is helping, selecting various items as –

Cheerleaders (*softly, hauntingly*)
Cheer girls, sneer girls,
wrapped in golden gear girls.
Leer girls, queer girls,
the spread a little fear girls.

Travis If you think I'm threatened by you, you're wrong. I'm Travis Flood. I was threatening people before you were born. Crowds used to part to let me through. People brought me presents to keep me in a good mood. I'm Travis Flood!

Rio, Miss Sulphur and Miss Kerosene laugh at Travis.

Miss Sulphur starts putting face powder on Miss Kerosene.

268

Rio continues sorting through make-up, but starts glancing at Travis as –

Cheerleaders
Glam girls, wham girls,
the just don't give a damn girls.
Sleek girls, freak girls,
the totally unique girls.

Travis If I so much as sneezed I'd receive get-well cards by the lorry load. People would lick my boots and wipe my arse and consider themselves lucky to have that privilege. I'm Travis Flood!

Rio, Miss Sulphur and Miss Kerosene laugh at Travis.

Miss Sulphur continues putting make-up on Miss Kerosene.

Rio stops sorting through make-up and gazes at Travis as –

Cheerleaders
Flooze girls, cruise girls,
we ain't got no taboos girls.
Boot girls, cute girls,
with a liking to pollute girls.

Travis When I raised my voice the whole of East London would collectively shit itself. A snap of my fingers meant kneecaps would fly.

Cheerleaders C-H-E-E-R-L-E-A-D-E-R-S! Cheerleaders!

Travis You expect *me* to be scared by *you*. Ha! You're nothing! Nothing!

Miss Sulphur indicates Miss Kerosene's make-up.

Miss Sulphur What d'you think, girl?

Rio Lipstick's too light.

Miss Sulphur You think?

Rio Try the deep blood-red – oh, what's it called?

Miss Kerosene Knuckleduster Glory.

Miss Sulphur takes lipstick from handbag.

Miss Sulphur I thought about using this colour. Then I thought, No! With Miss Kerosene's eyes it's got to be Crushed Foetus.

Putting lipstick on Miss Kerosene.

But now . . . Yes, girl! You're right.

Travis Is this all you are?

Rio A girl's image is important, Travis.

Travis Image! You don't know the meaning of the bloody word. In the heydays we had style. Sophistication. I had my suits made by the finest tailors down Savile Row. Shot-silk suits. When I wore them I looked a million dollars. People would beg to touch my sleeve. I had pizzazz. Pizzazz!

Miss Sulphur indicates Miss Kerosene's make-up.

Miss Sulphur Miss Sparks?

Rio Mascara could be heavier.

Miss Sulphur But don't you think with Miss Kerosene's eyes –?

Rio If you don't want my opinion, don't ask.

Miss Sulphur puts heavier mascara on Miss Kerosene.

Travis tuts and shakes his head.

Travis Bimbos dressed in kitchen foil.

Rio You don't bother me, Travis. Fuck your precious heydays

Pause.

Miss Sulphur Miss Sparks?

Rio Eh? . . . What?

Miss Sulphur Mascara?

Rio Yeah. Fine.

Miss Sulphur Don't sound too convinced.

Miss Kerosene Mirror.

Miss Sulphur hands Miss Kerosene face compact.

Miss Kerosene studies her reflection.

Miss Kerosene It's too much.

Miss Sulphur I agree.

Miss Kerosene Miss Sparks?

Rio . . . What? What?

Miss Kerosene You sure about the mascara?

Rio It's fine! Just . . . just leave it, will you.

Travis Mascara? Lipstick? Too thick? Not red enough? Pathetic.

Rio You don't understand, Travis. How can a man ever understand . . . ? Don't look at me like that! I'm warning you. Make-up. Hair. Gold. It means we'll never forget.

Travis Forget what?

Rio Saint Donna.

Slight pause.

Travis . . . Your mother.

Rio Aha! You see, girls! That's got his attention. Yes, Travis. My mum. Destroyed by a man. Saint Donna.

At Miss Sulphur and Miss Kerosene.

Fucking say, Amen, you two. What's wrong with you?

Miss Sulphur I was about to start on the nail varnish.

Rio Fuck the nail varnish! I'm talking about Saint Donna. Say, Amen! Quick! Amen.

Miss Sulphur Amen!

Miss Kerosene Amen!

Pause.

Rio Stop looking at me like that, Travis. Like Saint Donna means nothing. Like *I* mean nothing . . . Oh, I'll fucking teach you.

Before Travis has a chance to respond, Rio takes handkerchief from Travis's top pocket and shoves it in his mouth.

Rio One of Torchie's bandages, Miss Sulphur. Quick! Quick!

Miss Sulphur gives bandage to Rio, then returns to make-up.

Rio ties bandage round Travis's head, securing gag firmly.

Rio sits and stares at Travis.

Slight pause.

Rio You wanted me to tell you about myself, didn't you, Travis?

Picks up Travis's book and flicks through it.

The story of Rio Sparks . . . *The Girl with the Gold Mini-Skirt*! Ha! How's that sound, Travis? How'd you begin yours . . .

Reads from book.

'Chapter One . . . Once, long ago, I was born in a –'

The Cheerleaders make noises of derisive laughter.

That what you think your life is, Travis? Eh? All once-upon-a-time and rescuing a pretty princess. Well, my story ain't anything like that. Mine's a fairy-tale with spikes and acid. Listen! . . . Once upon a time I was born in a shit-hole called Bethnal Green.

The Cheerleaders make noises of approval.

Born in that room there. My mum . . . she was fourteen years old. You got that, Travis? Fourteen fucking years old. She screamed for hours giving birth to me. I ripped her like razors. There was so much blood. Mattress was dripping with it. Blood up the walls. On the light bulb. It turned the whole room red – Yeah! That's it! A blood-red room! And into this . . . this inferno came me. How's that for a fairy-story, eh?

Slight pause.

Chapter Two. My mum . . . she was buried. Grandad . . . he went crazy. Tried to kill himself. Jumped from the roof and cracked his head in two. Opened like a coconut, Travis. Blood poured out of his wound. Like a . . . a snake – Yeah! That's it! A snake! The snake crawled across the pavement . . . Up the stairs . . . Under that front door. Across the room. And up to Torchie as she rocked me in her arms. The snake touched Torchie's foot. It hissed, 'Your family is cursed.'

Miss Kerosene and Miss Sulphur clap and cheer.

Miss Kerosene Go on, girl! Next chapter!

Rio Three.

Pause.

Rio is seven years old. She wakes up one night. A noise. Very soft. She gets up and comes into this room. Moonlight. Tiny sounds get a little louder. Squeaking. Scraping. Rio looks round. There! The noises are coming from the cupboard under the sink.

Goes to the cupboard and looks inside.

A rat! It runs to the corner. Two eyes glaring at me. Bright red. And there . . . in a nest of torn newspaper. Baby rats. Five of them. Like pink jelly. Pink jelly with blue veins. And wriggling. Wriggling.

Miss Kerosene Kill them! Go on!

Rio I pour the bleach over them. They wriggle faster. Paws clutch. It goes on and on. Pour more bleach. But they won't die. Just wriggle and wriggle. Make it stop! Make it stop!

Miss Kerosene Stomp on them!

Rio I can't! Just watch and watch and . . .

Pause.

Miss Kerosene What's happening?

Rio They're dead.

Miss Kerosene Let me see!

Miss Sulphur It's just a story, you stupid cow!

Pause.

Miss Kerosene sits.

Slight pause.

Rio Chapter Four. Rio can't sleep. Every night, in the dark, she imagines a rat coming to kill her. Large mummy rat. To avenge her dead lumps of pink jelly. Rio screams in the dark. Torchie tries to comfort her. She tells me stories about my mum.

Miss Kerosene Saint Donna!

Miss Sulphur Saint Donna!

Rio You see, Travis. How these girls understand me? Don't look at me like that, Travis. There's still things you've got to know. I ain't finished yet.

Pause.

Chapter Five. Rio is ten years old. She's walking through the market. It's snowing. Nearly Christmas. Little fairy lights sparkling round shop windows. And around the stalls. People laughing. A radio. Jingle song. Smell of food. Chestnuts. Roast chestnuts. Tangerines. Apples. Oranges. And . . . what's that? Something cut in pieces. Never seen that before.

Miss Kerosene What's it look like?

Rio Green outside. Red inside.

Miss Sulphur Melon.

Rio A voice! Man. Stall-owner. 'Is that what it's called?' I say, 'A melon? Looks tasty . . . What you say? Would I like a bite? Well, yeah, but I ain't got any money . . . What? You'll give me a piece? For nothing? If I do what . . . ? Touch you where . . . ? Nah! Can't do that . . . Where you taking me? Back of your van! Smells of fruit.

Makes me giddy. All right, all right! I'm touching you!
You like that?' Touching! Smell lemons. Touch. Apples.
Touch . . .

Pause.

Afterwards I sit on a swing. It's still snowing.

Miss Kerosene Hope you've got your melon, girl.

Rio I bite into it. It crunches. Juice. Sweet. Red. Trickles
down my chin. Dribbles into my white dress. Like blood.
Bite again. Like eating a human heart.

*Miss Sulphur and Miss Kerosene gently murmur
approval.*

Slight pause.

Rio Chapter Six. Rio is lying in bed. Moonlight. Noise.
Mummy rat. Coming to get me. Wants to crawl into my
mouth when I'm asleep. Wants to eat my tongue. Crawl
down my throat. Into stomach. Eat guts. No! I won't
sleep. I'll stay awake all night! I'll never sleep again!
Sniff magic fairy-dust to keep me awake!

Pause.

Chapter Seven. Rio is older now. It's night. She's
standing on a corner. Street lights. Everything's orange.
Like there's a fire somewhere. Car pulls up. 'What you
want, mister? I'll do anything. I don't care.' Later. Stand
in the orange light again. Another car. 'What you want,
mister? I'll do anything. I don't care.' Later. Orange
light. Another car. 'I don't care.' Later. Orange. Car.
'Don't care.' Then I see . . . Look! The clouds whizz
across the sky! Flowers bloom and die. Time passes.
Years. Get older. My hands. Look! Tiny wrinkles. And
veins. On my face too. It all happens while I stand in
that orange light. Another car. 'What you want, mister?

I don't care . . . What's that? I'm too old. Fuck off, you bastard! Fuck off!'

Pause.

Chapter . . . what? Don't matter. Bed. Moonlight. Noise. Rat! Where? Find it.

Looks round room.

In here! No! Still hear it. Where?

Miss Kerosene Under the sink.

Miss Sulphur Rats keep going to the same place.

Rio You're right . . . The sound is getting louder and louder . . . Louder . . . Louder . . .

Opens cupboard under sink.

There! Biggest rat I've ever seen. Eyes red. Dark fur. Claws. It's running!

Miss Kerosene Where?

Rio Under the table!

Miss Kerosene Kill it!

Rio It's gone into a hole! Beside the cooker. Never noticed that before! Bastard rat! It'll never come out again! I'll make sure of that.

Rio starts looking for something.

Miss Sulphur What are you looking for now, girl?

Rio Matches!

Miss Kerosene throws matches at Rio.

Miss Kerosene Here!

Rio gets to her knees beside the cooker.

Miss Sulphur This is how the fire started, ain't it. You never told us this, girl.

Rio Flames licking up the gas cooker . . . the wall . . . sparks in the air . . . Beautiful, beautiful . . .

Miss Sulphur It's out of control, girl.

Rio Fire! Everywhere!

Miss Sulphur You've got to get out, girl! Quick! Wake Torchie!

Rio . . . Torchie!

   Pause.

Next chapter. In hospital. Torchie in bed. Tubes coming out her nose. Leg bandaged. Can't bear it. Me. I did this. 'Is she gonna die? Tell me!' Torchie moans. She's in pain. She's crying. No! I run. Out of the ward. Down the corridor. Out of the hospital. Orange light. I'm crying again. Clouds swirl. Run. Running from rats. Run. Running from red light bulb. Run. Room of blood. Run. Inferno. Run. Snake of blood. Run. 'You're cursed!' Run. Across the pavement. Run. Baby rats. Run. Pink jelly. Run. Wriggling. Run. Human hearts. Run. Sweet juice. Run. Blood on white dress. Run. 'What do you want, mister? I don't care.' Run. Rats. Run. I'm in the graveyard. There. Mum's grave. Help me. Help me. Help me.

Miss Sulphur Calm down, girl.

Rio That's . . . that's just what you said.

Miss Sulphur What d'you mean?

Rio You were in the graveyard. The two of you. We meet. You say . . .

Miss Sulphur . . . What's wrong?

Rio Rats. Blood. Heart. Help.

Miss Kerosene Jesus! What you on, girl?.

Rio There. In the sky. A swarm of insects. Look.
Millions of insects. Their wings are making humming
noises. Locusts. They're landing on everything. On all
the tombstones. Catch one. Squeeze. Yellow stuff spurts.
Lick it. Honey. Oh, Mum, Mum.

Miss Sulphur This your mum's grave, girl?

Rio Donna!

Miss Sulphur What was she like, girl? Calm down. Tell
us . . .

Slight pause.

Rio She . . . she had blonde hair.

Miss Sulphur What style?

Rio A pony-tail.

Slight pause.

Look. All the clouds forming together. Taking shape.
A girl. A fourteen-year-old girl. With blonde hair. Tied
in a pony-tail. Oh . . . it's Mum. And then . . . then
I realise. My Mum is a saint. All her suffering was not
in vain. She is the Saint of All the Damaged Girls Living
in the Ruins. Oh, yes. Yes. She's there for me. My life . . .
It means something. Saint Donna! Saint Donna!

Pause.

Miss Kerosene Feel better now, girl?

Rio . . . Yeah.

Miss Sulphur What's your name?

Rio Miss Sparks.

Miss Sulphur So call me . . . Miss Sulphur.

Miss Kerosene And me Miss Kerosene.

Rio The Cheerleaders are formed! Our gang! Cheer-leaders! And we talk more and more about Saint Donna. We work out the commandments of Saint Donna – Don't look like that, Travis. Girls! Come on, let's tell him the commandments! What's the first one, Miss Sulphur?

Miss Sulphur Always wear make-up.

Rio Amen!

Slight pause.

Say, Amen!

Miss Kerosene Amen!

Rio Second, Miss Kerosene?

Miss Kerosene Be . . . be . . .

Rio Blonde! Amen!

Miss Sulphur Amen!

Rio Third, Miss Sulphur?

Miss Sulphur Have a pony-tail!

Rio Good! Amen!

Miss Kerosene Amen!

Rio Fourth, Miss Kerosene?

Miss Kerosene Partake of chemicals?

Rio That's right, girl. Partake of chemicals. Amen!

Miss Sulphur Amen!

Rio Fifth, Miss Sulphur?

Miss Sulphur Partake of more chemicals.

Rio Lots of chemicals! Amen!

Miss Kerosene Amen!

Rio Sixth, Miss Kerosene?

Pause.

Rio . . . Wear.

Miss Kerosene . . . Wear?

Rio Wear gold . . .

Miss Kerosene Wear gold togs?

Rio Amen!

Miss Sulphur Amen!

Rio Miss Sulphur. Seventh! Come on!

Miss Sulphur Piss on men!

Rio Amen!

Miss Kerosene Amen!

Rio Miss Kerosene?

Slight pause.

Miss Kerosene Oh, I'm fucking bored with this now. Why can't we just smash his head in and be done with it?

Rio Tell Travis the eighth commandment. He'll think you don't know.

Miss Sulphur Who gives a fuck what he thinks?

Rio *I* do!

Miss Kerosene Well, I can't fucking remember.

Rio Dominate! The eighth is dominate! You should know this. We've gone over it a million fucking times. It's what the Cheerleaders believe.

Slight pause.

Ninth, Miss Sulphur?

Miss Sulphur Celebrate the ruins!

Rio Amen! And number ten is pray to Saint Donna. And the prayer goes . . . Girls? Come on! Please!

The Girls Our Saint Donna who are in the Queendom, Golden be thy name in the ruins as it is in the Queendom above . . .

Miss Sulphur and Miss Kerosene stop saying prayer.

Rio Deliver us from men and encourage our sins as we forgive – come on, girls – no one that sins against us. For thine is – girls! Come on! Don't let me down! – the Queendom, the make-up and the pony-tail. For ever and ever. Amen.

Travis is struggling, trying to say something.

Pause.

Rio starts removing his gag.

Miss Sulphur What you doing?

Rio He wants to say something.

Miss Sulphur Who's bothered?

Travis's gag is removed.

Travis Fantasies. Dreams. Lies. That's all your life is. Nothing but . . . hallucinations. Just like you. All your . . . partaking of chemicals – look what it's turned you into! Phantoms. Zombies. Nothing.

Pause.

Why you keeping me here? Eh? To hurt me? Well, you ain't doing a very good job. In the heydays we knew how to hurt. Oh, yes. *I* knew how to hurt. Me, Travis Flood. I was threatening people before you were born. When I raised my voice the whole of East London would collectively shit itself. A snap of my fingers meant knee-caps would fly. Oh, I've done things. Bad things. But you . . . you're all talk. And talking is nothing. It's what you do to skin that matters.

Miss Kerosene I've done bad things to skin.

Travis I've done worse.

Miss Kerosene What?

Travis . . . My secret.

Miss Kerosene Tell me!

Travis No.

Miss Kerosene You fucking better!

Travis Or what?

Miss Kerosene I'll hurt you bad.

Travis Aha! At last! *Now* we're getting somewhere. Look! There's a cigar on the table! Pick it up! Go on!

Pause.

Go on.

Rio Do it, girl.

Miss Kerosene picks up cigar.

Travis That's it. Now light it.

Pause.

283

Rio Do it.

Miss Kerosene lights it.

Travis Oh, better and better! Now . . . you don't need me to tell you what to do, do you? There's something you want me to tell you. I refuse. You've got the cigar. I've got the skin. Make me.

Pause.

Do it!

Very casually, Miss Kerosene stubs the cigar against Travis's face.

Travis Oh, you'll have to do better than that.

Pause.

Rio Do it again.

Miss Kerosene burns Travis.

Travis That won't make me tell you.

Miss Kerosene burns Travis again.

Miss Kerosene Tell me!

Travis Never.

Miss Sulphur takes cigar from Miss Kerosene and burns Travis.

Travis Is . . . is this the best you can do?

Miss Kerosene and Miss Sulphur take turns burning Travis.

Travis I'll never tell! Ahh! Hear that, Rio? And you can't – Ahh! – make me . . . You call this . . . hurting? Ahh! This is nothing! You can't even get passionate about hurting someone – Ahhh! In the heydays grown men

284

would be in ecstasy when – Ahhh! – inflicting pain! But this is child's play. Just like your stupid Saint Donna –

Rio grabs scissors from table.

Miss Kerosene and Miss Sulphur stand back.

Travis Do it, Rio! Wake up and do it!

Rio spreads blades of scissors in the air.

She approaches Travis, aiming blades at his face.

Travis So . . . you'd hurt a defenceless old man, would you? Eh?

Then . . . just as Rio is about to strike Travis –

Travis It's Saturday night.

Rio freezes.

Pause.

Rio goes to strike again –

Travis I'm wearing my black suit.

Rio freezes again.

Slowly, she calms.

She lowers scissors.

Rio Let's hear it then. It's Saturday night. You're wearing your black suit. Go on.

Travis There's a lily in my lapel. I always wear a lily. I'm the man with the white lily. I look immaculate. I'm with my two boys. They're wearing black suits too. We're out collecting money. That's what we do every Saturday night. I'm standing in front of a large building. Can you see it? There's neon lights. Very bright. It's the last stop of the evening. A cinema.

*Travis's words are beginning to touch a nerve with
Rio now.*

Travis I go to the projection box. That's where the man
will be. The man I get my money from. Look! There!
The projector is showing a film. Flickering light
everywhere.

Miss Sulphur What a boring pile of –

Rio Shut up!

Miss Kerosene Stab him!

Rio raises the scissors at Miss Kerosene.

Pause.

*Miss Sulphur and Miss Kerosene start looking at nail
varnish.*

Rio Go on, Travis.

Travis Here's the man! Look! The man who runs the
cinema. 'Where's my fucking money?' He's looking very
nervous. Face covered with sweat. 'What's that? Speak
up . . . You ain't got it? Stop snivelling! I don't want
your excuses. I'll hurt you, you fucking bastard.' My
boys grab hold of him. Twist his arm. The man's
screaming. 'Break it! Snap his fucking arm off!' Look
at him! He's on the floor. I'll hear his bones crack in a
minute –

Looks round as if catching sight of something.

Someone's walked into the room. It's the man's daughter.
She's looking at me. Those large eyes. 'Let go of him!'
The girl rushes up to her dad. 'Don't worry. He ain't
hurt bad. Not yet. But next time . . .!' I walk out of the
projection box. My boys are following me. We leave the
cinema. Go to the car. And then – those eyes again. The

286

girl. 'What d'you want? Speak up. . . . Why am I hurting your dad? Well . . . why don't you get in the car and I'll tell you.' My boys are laughing. They know what's on my mind. 'Keep watch you two! Now – get in the car.' Oh, the girl is so beautiful. She has long hair in a pony-tail. She's getting in the car. Her name is . . . d'you know her name?

Rio . . . Can you hear him?

Slight pause.

Miss Sulphur? Miss Kerosene? Can you hear what he's saying?

Rio looks round at Miss Sulphur and Miss Kerosene.

They are engrossed with the nail varnish.

Rio What . . . what you doing?

Miss Sulphur It's a new colour. Clawed Face.

Rio You ain't listening to him!

Miss Sulphur What's got into you, girl?

Miss Kerosene Ooo, just look at this colour!

Pause.

Rio Both of you . . . you can go now.

Miss Sulphur What?

Slight pause.

Rio Wait for me in the graveyard.

Miss Sulphur But what about –

Rio I'll deal with him. Alone.

Miss Sulphur starts packing up make-up.

Miss Sulphur If that's the way you want it. But, next time, don't go calling for help if you don't fucking want any.

Miss Kerosene indicates her nail varnish.

Miss Kerosene Just tell me if you like this colour.

Miss Sulphur Don't waste your breath, girl. She's in one of her moods again. I'm warning you, Miss Sparks. You'll push it too far one day.

Miss Sulphur and Miss Kerosene leave.

Long pause.

Rio sits next to Travis.

Rio We're in the car.

Travis Your dad owes me money. That's why I hurt him. What d'you say to that?

Rio He . . . he can't afford to pay.

Travis Then he gets hurt some more. And so does your mum.

Rio No. Please.

Travis Maybe you can help.

Rio What? I'll do anything.

Travis Come closer, Donna.

Rio Will . . . will you stop asking them for money?

Travis Yes.

Rio And hurting them?

Travis Yes, yes.

Pause.

Rio What . . . what are you doing?

Travis Relax.

Rio It hurts.

Travis Shut up! Do you want me to hurt your mum and dad?

Rio No.

Travis Then do as you're told. And you mustn't tell anyone. You hear? Not your mum. Not your dad. No one.

Rio You're making me bleed.

Travis I'm kissing your lips.

Rio I'm crying.

Pause.

Afterwards I run out of the car. I'm hysterical –

Travis No, no. You're very calm. You walk back to the cinema. I watch you from the car. I'm waiting for you to look back. But you don't. Not once. You go into the cinema. The door swings shut behind you. I never see you again.

Rio And I . . . die.

Travis I never knew that. I'd run away by then. Left it all behind.

Rio You go to America.

Travis Yes.

Rio With your fortune.

Travis There ain't no fortune. Never was. I go there with fuck-all. And that's how it stays. No swimming-pool.

No Cadillac. No speedboat. Nothing. Just an endless succession of petty jobs. And always moving. And everywhere I go I change my name. Invent new stories about myself. In the end, I begin to forget who I am. Who I was. So I write a book . . . Yes! I wore a black suit! Crowds parted to let me through! A snap of my fingers meant kneecaps would fly! That's it. In a paradise called Bethnal Green they will remember. They will remember who I am. I have to publish the book myself. It costs me nearly everything I've got. The rest goes on a plane ticket. And this suit. I'm the man with the white lily again. I come back here. Visit all my old haunts. But . . . hardly anyone remembers me. One old tramp laughs and says I look like a gangster. And that's it. Except . . . in a graveyard I meet a girl. We talk for a while. She says she's heard about me. We arrange to meet later. She gives me her address. But I arrive early. I talk to her grandmother. She tells me stories. And . . . I piece together another story. A story the grandmother ain't even aware of. A story about me.

Pause.

Now I know who I am.

Very long pause.

Slowly, Rio stands.

Rio approaches Travis, holding scissors.

Travis flinches away.

But –

Rio cuts the rope tying Travis to the chair.

Pause.

Rio You best go before Torchie gets back.

Travis Will you tell her?

Rio No.

Slowly, Travis stands.

Pause.

Travis moves towards Rio.

Rio stares at him.

Travis stands in front of Rio.

Slight pause.

Travis strokes Rio's face gently.

He leans forward to kiss her cheek.

Rio spits in his face.

Slight pause.

Travis goes to door and opens it.

Travis Goodbye, Miss Sparks.

Rio Goodbye, Mr Flood.

Travis exits.

Rio is very still.

Very, very long pause.

Torchie enters.

Torchie Mr Flood gone, Baby Rio?

Rio . . . Yeah.

Torchie notices the chair Travis had been tied to.

Torchie Lor'struth, looks like he had his fun. Hope he was generous.

Takes off coat, sits and starts removing bandage from leg.

Torchie I said to Grandad Sparks, 'Guess who's back at our house? Mr Flood! Mr Flood from the heydays!' Thought that might cause a reaction. But no. Not a flicker.

Slight pause.

Then again . . . what would I do if he suddenly woke up. After all, he's been asleep so long. Years and years. So much has changed. If he woke up he might wonder who we are.

Fade to blackout.